CHILE: The Pinochet Decade
The Rise and Fall of the Chicago Boys

LAB

Latin America Bureau
Research and action on Latin America

First published in Great Britain in 1983 by

Latin America Bureau (Research and Action) Ltd
Amwell Street
London EC1R 1UL

Published with the assistance of:

Methodist World Development Action Fund
Chile Solidarity Campaign
Chile Committee for Human Rights
Chile Democratico
Catholic Institute for International Relations
Latin American Working Group, Toronto

The views expressed however, are those of the authors

Written by Phil O'Brien and Jackie Roddick
Additional material from Jon Barnes and James Painter
Design by Jan Brown Designs
Map by Michael Green
Typeset, printed and bound by Russell Press Ltd, Nottingham
Trade distribution in UK by Third World Publications

Authors' Acknowledgement

Thanks are due to the Institute of Latin American Studies of the University
of Glasgow, and to the Social Science Research Council, which funded two
research projects on Chile in 1979 and 1980 and to John Mackenzie and
Nigel Haworth, our fellow researchers.

Contents

Chile

PERU

Iquique

BOLIVIA

Antofagasta

PARAGUAY

ARGENTINA

Copiapó

BRAZIL

La Serena

SOUTH PACIFIC OCEAN

Valparaíso

SANTIAGO
METROPOLITAN REGION
Rancagua

URUGUAY

Talca

Concepción

Temuco

Puerto Montt

SOUTH ATLANTIC OCEAN

Coihaique

Aisén del General
Carlos Ibáñez del
Campo

ISLAS MALVINAS/
FALKLAND ISLANDS

Magallanes
y Antártica
Chilena

Punta Arenas

Canal Beagle

1 Chile in Brief

Statistics

Area   292,257 sq. miles
(UK = 94,200 sq. miles)

Population

Total	11.49 million (1982)
Growth	1.6% (annual average rate 1970-81)
Urban	81.5% (1980)
Distribution	77% live in 'middle Chile' (the area between Copiapo and Concepción) which covers 18% of the total land area.

**Principal
Towns**   Greater Santiago - 4,039,000; Viña del Mar - 290,000; Valparaiso - 267,000; Talcahuana - 209,000; Concepción - 206,000; Antofagasta - 167,000; Temuco - 162,000. (1982)

The People   Race   Largely *mestizo* (of mixed Indian and Spanish stock), with approx. 20 per cent direct descendants of European immigrants. An estimated

1

		250,000-600,000 descendants of the Mapuche Indians live in the south of Chile, especially around Temuco.
	Language	Spanish
	Religion	Roman Catholic
Economy	GDP (1981)	Total US$18,636 million
		Per Capita US$1,675
	Trade (1981)	Exports US$3,960 million
		Imports US$6,558 million
	Principal Exports (1981)	Minerals 58.0% (copper 43%, iron ore 4.1%, molybdenum 3.8%); industrial/processed goods 32.7%; agricultural products 9.3%
	Inflation	1978 40%
		1979 33%
		1980 35%
		1981 9%
		1982 21%
	Foreign Debt (US$ billions)	1979 8.3
		1980 9.8
		1981 13.1
		1982 17.5
	Debt Characteristics (1982)	Due in 1983/4: US$3.5 billion Total Debt as a % of exports: 85% Total Debt per capita: US$1,550
	Public Spending (1979)	Military US$956 million
		Education US$764 million
		Health US$458 million
	Unemployment (1982)	23.9% 27.9%, including workers on Minimum Employment Programme.
	Minimum wage (1982)	US$69 (at official rate of 75 pesos = 1 dollar) per month

2

Literacy (1979)	94%
Health	Life expectancy at birth: 65.7 years (1975-80); Infant mortality: 38 per 1,000 live births (1979); One doctor per 1,120 inhabitants (1980).

Sources: Banco Central de Chile, Instituto Nacional de Estadisticas, Lloyds Bank, World Bank Debt Tables 1982/3, Inter-American Development Bank, World Military and Social Expenditures 1982 (Ruth Leger Sivard).

Chronology

1541   Foundation of Santiago by Pedro de Valdivia.

1818   Chile achieves independence from Spain under leadership of Bernardo O'Higgins and Argentinian San Martín. O'Higgins becomes first president (*Director Supremo*) of Chile.

1833   New constitution, introduced by Diego Portales, establishes strongly-centralized and authoritarian state.

1879-1883   Bolivia and Peru defeated by Chile in the War of the Pacific. Bolivia loses access to the sea, and Chile gains possession of the Atacama desert, main source of the world's supply of nitrates.

1891   Defeat of President Jose Manuel Balmaceda in brief civil war.

1907   Massacre of 3,000 miners by troops after demonstration in nitrate port of Iquique.

1920   Arturo Alessandri elected as president.

1922   Communist Party of Chile officially formed.

1927-1931   Military dictatorship of Colonel Carlos Ibañez.

1932   12-day 'Socialist Republic' of Colonel Marmaduke Grove. Arturo Alessandri elected as president for second time.

1933   Foundation of Chilean Socialist Party.

1938   Election of Popular Front government, with a programme of state investment and state protection for national industry, under joint banner of Radical, Communist and Socialist Parties.

1948   *Ley Maldita*, or the 'Evil Law', bans the Communist Party.

1952-1958   Second administration of Carlos Ibañez.

1958   Salvador Allende, presidential candidate for the Popular Action Front (FRAP), loses to National Party candidate, Jorge Alessandri, by 33,000 votes.

1964	Eduardo Frei, Christian Democrat candidate, wins election with 56 per cent of the vote, offering 'revolution in liberty' as an alternative to Marxist socialism.
1970	Salvador Allende, candidate for Popular Unity, wins presidential elections with 36 per cent of the vote, and becomes first ever elected Marxist president.
1973	Military coup. Military junta composed of Leigh, Merino, Pinochet and Mendoza takes power; Popular Unity parties banned; others suspended. National trade union confederation CUT dissolved. Congress dissolved; *Comité Pro Paz* created by Catholic and Lutheran Churches to deal with victims of repression. Junta organizes legislative committees: army controls defence and Leniz named minister of economy.
1974	DINA, Chile's secret police, created, solely responsible to Pinochet, who now becomes officially head of junta; *El Mercurio* outlines two alternative measures to reduce inflation: gradualism or economic 'shock treatment'; Christian Democrat advisers leave government; ban on union elections. Wage freeze continues, but old law of contract reinstated against employers' opposition; General Prats murdered in Buenos Aires. Miguel Enriquez, leader of MIR, killed in Santiago; *El Mercurio* comes out in favour of shock treatment in November. Privatization of banks announced; Pinochet becomes president of Chile in December.
1975	General Bonilla killed in air crash. Friedman and Harberger visit Chile to support 'shock treatment' to reduce inflation; cabinet reshuffle, consolidating 'Chicago' hold on government. Minister of finance Cauas announces introduction of 'shock treatment'; Movement of National Unity created by Declaration of Codegua, in face of growing economic emergency and world hostility to Chile; arrest of trade unionists from El Salvador copper mine. Ministry of interior (responsible to Pinochet) takes over control of trade union affairs from General Diaz and air force; Academy for National Security created; Leigh declares social cost of Chicago Plan too high; assassination attempt on left-wing Christian Democrat exile Bernardo Leighton in Rome; Comité Pro Paz dissolved, Vicaría de Solidaridad created; withdrawal of British ambassador after torture of Sheila Cassidy, a British doctor.
1976	Cabinet reshuffle: air force General Diaz replaced by Chicago supporter Sergio Fernandez at ministry of labour; *El Mercurio* reports 20 minute strike attempt at Chuquicamata copper mine; Group of Ten right-wing Christian Democrat trade union leaders emerge into open with public letter to Fernandez; Letelier murdered in Washington; CNS made up of Marxists and left-wing Christian Democrats makes its first public appearance with

another open letter to Fernandez; pro-government union confederation UNTRACH formed; Chile withdraws from Andean Pact.

1977 All political parties made illegal; British mediation awards Chile legal title to three disputed islands in Beagle Channel; DINA disbanded in wake of Letelier scandal, replaced by CNI; Bardon (Chicago supporter) president of central bank, says Chile will increase its foreign debt to speed up battle against inflation; Friedrich Von Hayek, father of free-market 'Chicago model' visits Chile; economics minister De Castro announces reduction of virtually all tariffs to 10 per cent.

1978 State of siege changed to state of emergency; Fernandez becomes minister of interior. Hernan Cubillos becomes minister of foreign relations with mandate to end Chile's diplomatic isolation; members of US AFL-CIO visit Chile at the invitation of the Group of Ten; Leigh and eight other air force chiefs retired. Matthei becomes chief of air force and new member of junta; Pinochet holds fourth mass meeting with trade union leaders organized by *Secretario de los Gremios*; Manuel Contreras indicted for murder of Letelier. Argentina calls up reserves and sends troops to Chilean border. Pinochet gives in to demands for union elections, and allows them in private sector. CNS federations dissolved; Vatican's offer to mediate the Beagle issue is accepted, after church in Chile and Argentina organizes protest demonstrations against war; US unions announce plan to organize a transport boycott of Chilean goods; first public discussion of the 'disappeared' of 1973 after bodies are found at Lonquen. Cabinet reshuffle: Fernandez's deputy at the labour ministry is replaced by Chicago Boy Jose Piñera, completing the Chicago revolution.

1979 Piñera promises restoration of trade union rights, an end to police surveillance of trade unions. Proposed US union boycott is lifted; collective bargaining begins for first time since the coup; size of US Embassy in Santiago cut as protest over government's failure to extradite Contreras.

1980 Government wins strike at El Teniente copper mine, seen as a victory for Chicago-style Labour Plan; protest march by student doctors unable to get jobs; Pinochet's trip to Philippines cancelled hours before his arrival; Cubillos is sacked as foreign minister; in first free university elections, opposition students win two thirds of vote; civil police investigating tax frauds by DINA officers receive death threats; assassination of intelligence officer, Vergara, leads to new *duro* gains in security, as Mena, a supporter of liberalization, is replaced by *duro* General Gordon at CNI. Ex-DINA head Contreras welcomes appointment; disillusioned Fatherland and Freedom leader founds Popular Nationalist Movement, capitalizing on discontent of small farmers in south;

5

opposition wins easily in first genuine union elections. Plebiscite on new constitution, Pinochet wins by large majority; *duros* given go-ahead to create new Civic-Military Movement to support government.

1981

Feb. Reagan lifts Carter restrictions on US government finance to Chile.

March New constitution comes into effect. ODEPLAN announces plans to break up state monopolies.

April Four-week strike at El Teniente.

May Jorge Ross' business empire, based on CRAV sugar refinery, collapses, sending shock waves through financial community.

July CNS leaders Bustos and Guzman imprisoned.

Sept. Open disputes between *duros* and *blandos* in government over new mining code. Four opposition politicians expelled for trying to create a political force of the centre.

Nov. Government takes over four banks and four finance companies, arresting three prominent financiers.

Dec. Dispute among *blandos*. Chicago Boy Piñera, minister of mining, calls for a 10 to 15 per cent devaluation and higher import tariffs. He is replaced. Pinochet says Chicago model to continue, but *duro* General Danus brought into ODEPLAN as a gesture to economic nationalists.

1982

Jan. Eduardo Frei, leader of the Christian Democrats, dies. Thousands march behind funeral procession chanting anti-government slogans.

Feb. Moderate trade union leader Tucapel Jimenez, of the public employees' union ANEF, assassinated after calling for a united trade union front.

April Pinochet declares Chile neutral in Falklands/Malvinas conflict despite constant rumours of secret pacts between Chile and the UK; cabinet re-shuffle; Fernandez is replaced at the interior ministry by Montero Marx, and *duros* Generals Danus and Frez become minister of the economy and minister of ODEPLAN respectively.

May Entire executive committee of the CNS arrested; Edwards takes over the editorship of *El Mercurio*.

June Peso devalued by 18 per cent, despite prior denials.

July IMF offers standby credit of US$1 billion to prevent collapse of banking system; guerrilla attack blacks out Valparaiso for four hours.

August Central bank steps in to buy private sector's bad debts of US$1 billion; cabinet reshuffle, Danus and Frez resign, and Rolf Lüders, Chicago economist and head of BHC business empire,

	assumes ministries of economy and finance; unemployment officially stands at 24 per cent.
Sept.	Four different exchange rates are introduced in an effort to protect banks and business empires with huge private debts; demonstrations in Santiago and Valparaiso, 70 arrested.
Nov.	CNS offices raided; national debt reaches US$14 billion; negotiations begin with IMF for US$850 million loan.
Dec. 2-3	Massive demonstrations in Santiago against government economic policies; CNS leader Manuel Bustos and construction workers leader Hector Cuevas, together with Carlos Podlech of the right-wing Wheat Growers Association expelled.
8	Hunger strike by relatives of the disappeared.
15	Co-ordinated demonstrations in Santiago, Valparaiso and Concepción, 200 arrested; police raids on shanty-towns in Santiago, 1,500 arrested; four main trade union organizations present a single charter of demands to the government.

1983

Jan.	IMF agrees package of US$850 million; government take over nine key banks and financial institutions; BHC empire forced into liquidation by government; nine former congressmen of the National Party criticize regime's economic policies.
Feb.	90-day moratorium announced pending agreement on the rescheduling of US$2.8 billion debt; cabinet re-shuffle, Carlos Caceros beomes fourth finance minister in 12 months; press censorship re-introduced; General Sinclair takes over as Pinochet's second-in-command.
March	Caceres seeks extra US$1.2 billion loan from commercial banks; broad opposition front of political parties (except Communists) formed; 200 arrested after clashes between police and demonstrators; import tariffs doubled to 20 per cent; 'democratic manifesto' signed by broad spectrum of parties.
April	SNA warns that free market policies in agriculture have led to a massive shortage in basic foods.
May 1	May Day demonstrations in Santiago, 76 arrested.
11	National day of protest called by the copper workers trade union (CTC) attracts widespread support from all sectors. Two civilians killed, 150 injured and 600 arrested; Pinochet advocates the formation of pro-government civilian-military movement; US$480 million bridging loan requested to meet short-term cash shortage.
June 14	Second day of national protest; more than a thousand arrests, and three shot dead; CTC president, Rodolfo Seguel also arrested.
17	24-hour protest strike held by copper workers.
22	Adolfo Quinteros, leader of the truckowners federation, arrested.
23-26	General Strike.

| July 10 | Three leaders of the Christian Democrats, including Gabriel Valdes, arrested and held for five days. |
| 12 | Third day of national protest; army used to clear the streets for the first time since the coup. |

Political Parties

After the coup all parties forming the *Unidad Popular* (Popular Unity) were banned, together with the MIR. All the remaining parties, the National Party, the Christian Democrats, and two small fascist groups, were considered 'in recess', and in March 1977 they were also dissolved. Since then no political parties have been officially allowed to participate in Chilean politics. Those parties which existed prior to the coup and are known to exist either in Chile or in exile in May 1983 are:

Popular Unity Parties

Partido Comunista de Chile (Communist Party)

Formed out of the Socialist Workers Party and officially founded in 1922 by Luis Emilio Recabarren. A Marxist-Leninist party, it has historically enjoyed a strong presence in the working class and trade union movement. Strongly pro-Soviet in ideology. Formed Popular Front of 1938 with Socialist and Radical parties, and was banned from 1948-1958. One of the main forces behind the formation of Popular Unity in 1969. It pursued a moderate line, including the pursuit of an alliance with the Christian Democrats all through the Allende period, which led to strong disagreements with the MIR and the left wing of the Socialist party. Official policy after the coup was 'to retreat in order to save the cadres and the organization'. Believed to have considerable presence in the CNS. After 1980 plebiscite joined forces with the MIR in advocating armed opposition to the Pinochet government as a viable tactic. Proposes establishment of provisional government to replace Pinochet.
Leader: Luis Corvalan (in exile).

Partido Socialista de Chile (Socialist Party)

Founded in 1933, the other main Marxist party with a large working class base. Affiliated to no international grouping. Throughout its history, the party has suffered numerous divisions. From 1948 onwards, two broad currents, the 'revolutionary' (who advocate an

8

immediate transition to socialism) and the more moderate or 'populist' have emerged. Salvador Allende, usually regarded as a moderate, stood as Socialist Party candidate in 1952, 1958 and 1964, and finally won in 1970. Through the Popular Unity years, Allende and his supporters tended to share Communist Party positions, while the group led by Carlos Altamirano advocated a more radical line. Heavily repressed after the coup, the party has suffered badly from a series of disputes, splits and lack of communication between the party in Chile and the leadership in exile. The two most important groups are led by Clodomiro Almeyda (foreign secretary in the Popular Unity government), which has preserved an underground apparatus in Chile, and (up until 1981) Carlos Altamirano (ex-secretary general of the party), which rejects the Eastern European model of socialism — the latter is now led by Jorge Arrate (in exile). There are several other groups within the Socialist Party, the majority of which support the Altamirano faction.

Movimiento de Acción Popular Unido (MAPU) (Movement for United Popular Action)

Formed in 1969 as a left-wing breakaway from the Christian Democrats, after disagreement over the latter's agrarian reform. Supporter of Popular Unity, its first secretary general, Jacques Chonchol, became minister of agriculture in the Allende government. At its first congress of 1970 declared itself a Marxist party. After March 1973 elections, the party split into MAPU-OC (*Obrero-campesino,* worker-peasant), which supported Communist Party positions and MAPU, which advocated more revolutionary positions. Leaders: Jaime Gazmuri (MAPU-OC), Oscar Garreton (MAPU).

Izquierda Cristiana (Christian Left)

Broke away from Christian Democrats in June 1971 after electoral pact between Christian Democrats and National Party. Non-Marxist party. Supporter of Popular Unity.
Leader: Luis Maera (in exile).

Partido Radical (Radical Party)

Formed in 1862 as a reaction against oligarchic domination of the Central Valley landowners. Historically its political base has come from white-collar workers and state employees. Formed the Popular Front of 1938 with the Socialist and Communist Parties. Won elections of 1938, 1942 and 1946. In 1969 minority of party split to form *Democracia Radical* (which supported the National Party

candidate in 1970), while the majority of the party supported the Popular Unity. In September 1971, the anti-Marxist *Partido de Izquierda Radical* (Radical Left Party) was formed which later left the Popular Unity in 1972.
Leaders: Anibal Palma/Anselmo Sule.

In March 1981 the **Convergencia Socialista** (Socialist Accord) was officially formed, which grouped together the Altamirano faction of the Socialist Party, MAPU, MAPU-OC, one sector of the Christian left, and independent socialists who proposed an alliance with moderate forces, but not the Communist Party nor the MIR.

Other main parties

Movimiento de Izquierda Revolucionario (MIR) (Movement of the Revolutionary Left)

Critical of the electoral orientation of the Socialist Party, a group of students split from the party in 1963. They formed the MIR in 1965 with a guerrilla orientation under the inspiration of the Cuban revolution. Has advocated the armed struggle since the time of its foundation. Clandestine in 1969, it did not participate in the elections of 1970. Heavily critical of reformist elements within the Popular Unity Government. Severely damaged after the coup with the death of general secretary Miguel Enriquez. Recent acts of sabotage in Chile confirm continued presence of the MIR. They now have a working relationship with the Communist Party.
Leader: Andres Pascal Allende.

Partido Democrático-Cristiano (Christian Democrat Party)

Founded in 1957 by an amalgam of the National Falange (a breakaway group from the Conservative Party in 1937) and the Social Christian Party. Promoted by the US in the era of the 'Alliance for Progress', its leader Eduardo Frei became president in 1964, as the proponent of the 'revolution in liberty', an alternative to Marxist socialism. Apart from the backing of the Catholic Church, the party has traditionally had the support of some industrialists, the urban poor, the unemployed and some peasant sectors. The party suffered internal divisions which led to certain sectors supporting the Pinochet coup, while other sections broke from the party and supported Popular Unity. The right-wing faction was slowly pushed into outright opposition to Pinochet when it became clear that the army intended to stay in power. By 1980 Frei and the party were leading the

moderate opposition to the plebiscite on the constitution. After Frei's death, Gabriel Valdes became new leader and both wings of the party have united against the present regime.
Leader: Gabriel Valdes.

Partido Nacional (National Party)

Formed in 1966 as a fusion of the old Conservative and Liberal Parties. Put up candidate, Jorge Alessandri, in 1970 elections and came second with 34.9 per cent of the vote. Vehemently opposed to Popular Unity and supported military coup from early 1973. In January 1983 nine ex-congressmen of National Party came out openly against the Pinochet government.

Trade Unions

After the coup in 1973 the main trade union organization, the CUT *(Central Unica de Trabajadores)* was dissolved and all unions were put under government control. Since then, massive repression, large-scale unemployment and a sharp decline in wages have led to enormous difficulties in re-organizing. Labour legislation, especially the Labour Plan of 1979, has aimed at keeping the trade union movement atomized and powerless. The following federations existed in Chile in May 1983:

CNS (Coordinadora Nacional Sindical) (National Co-ordinating Committee of Workers)

Loose grouping of Marxist and left-wing Christian Democrat unions. Made its first public appearance in September 1976 with an open letter to the then minister of labour, Fernandez. Formally banned in October 1978, though still active. Made a direct appeal to Pinochet in June 1981 for democratic reforms in the economy and labour organizations, and was instrumental in organizing mass demonstrations and strikes in early months of 1983. Membership includes miners, construction, textile and metallurgical workers as well as two peasant unions. It is the largest union federation with an estimated membership of more than 400,000 in 1980.
President: Manuel Bustos (expelled from Chile December 1982).
Secretary: Alamiro Guzman.

UDT (Unión Democrática de Trabajadores) (Democratic Workers Union, formerly known as the Group of Ten)

Led by a group of right-wing Christian Democrats, the Group of Ten

initially supported the government's policies and represented it at the annual ILO meetings. In May 1976 the group moved away from the government with the publication of open letters critical of their labour policies. Since then they have followed a more moderate line than the CNS. Membership includes dockers, truck drivers, bus drivers, some civil servants and two peasant unions. Estimated membership of 130,000 in 1980. Has strong international links with AFL-CIO, which produced US threat to boycott Chilean goods in 1978.
President: Eduardo Rios.

FUT (Frente Unitario de Trabajadores) (United Workers Front)

Established under the sponsorship of regional Christian Democrat unions, with a more left-wing slant than the Group of Ten (UDT). Membership includes taxi drivers, some local government employees and truck drivers. Smallest of federations.

CEPCH (Confederación de Empleados Particulares de Chile) (Federation of Private Sector Employees).

Left the Group of Ten after its decision to court the AFL-CIO. More confined to union problems, with membership of predominately white-collar workers. No formal international links. Estimated membership of 22,000 in 1980.
Leader: Federico Mujica.

Two of the most important sectoral unions are:
CTC (Confederación de Trabajadores del Cobre) (Federation of Copper Workers).

Groups together 24,000 workers in key copper sector. One of main forces behind recent strikes and demonstrations.
President: Rodolfo Seque. Vice-President: Hugo Estivales.

ANEF (Agropación Nacional de Empleados Fiscales) (National Association of Public Sector Employees).
Leader: Hernol Flores.

On 21 May 1983 all the above federations agreed to support the **Comando Nacional de Trabajadores** (National Workers Command).

UNTRACH (Unión Nacional de Trabajadores Chilenos) (National Union of Chilean Workers)

Created by the government in October 1976 to collaborate with

12

official labour policies, and based on the government-controlled copper confederation. After the Labour Plan of 1979, has withdrawn support from government. Membership includes banking unions, health workers, and nitrate workers. No international affiliation.

2 New and Old Extremisms

'Old Fascism' versus 'New Monetarism'

A decade after the September 1973 coup which brought down the socialist government of President Allende, we are in a position to understand the real significance of those tragic events. The coup saw the emergence of a new generation of right-wing activists who were committed to a brand-new right-wing ideology. This ideology, 'monetarism', the 'new economic orthodoxy', or 'libertarianism', has in the ten years since the coup imposed a new *laissez-faire* regime on the country which has elevated the market into the dominant force in all areas of life. This has been achieved despite opposition from many of the professional associations or *gremios* that played such an important part in Allende's downfall by creating a climate of hysteria and insecurity which paved the way for the coup. The *gremios* had sought a centrally directed fascist or corporatist project for the country's future.

In contemporary Chile fascism and monetarism are both allies and enemies, but it is important to distinguish between them. The Pinochet regime has often been labelled fascist, both by Latin American supporters of Popular Unity and by Europeans who would like the regime to be held in the kind of opprobrium which European fascism earned for itself after the massacre of the Jews. As a label it is clearly wrong. There are people in the Chilean government or near to it who would like to revive corporatist traditions, but they are its second-class citizens.

Like the presently fashionable monetarist orthodoxy, fascism in its day was an ideology imported into Latin America. It provided the basis for a broad-ranging fraternal brotherhood whose geographical spread we can occasionally trace today through the persistent rumours of German nazis still hiding in Brazil, Argentina, Paraguay and Bolivia. Some of the figures in this network have played a truly horrific role as the torturers and secret policemen of the new liberal capitalist order in Chile. One thinks, for instance, of *Colonia Dignidad*, the German settlement in Temuco in the south of Chile, used as a grave for the 'disappeared' by the Chilean military after 1973.

Both these ideologies have their roots in one of the periodic economic crises which seem to be almost a necessary part of a healthy capitalist system. Such crises give capitalism a chance to get rid of out-of-date businesses at the margins of profitability. At the same time, they provide a justification for eliminating social arrangements which no longer suit the needs of profitability in the modern world, and enable new experiments to take place. Fascism and monetarism, which both offer new patterns for the entire social order, are recipes for such experiments.

That is where their similarities end. Fascism is an extreme form of economic nationalism, extending state intervention in the economy while offering a cast-iron guarantee to the local capitalist class against any form of socialist takeover. It believes in organized social forces to represent the different sectoral interests at work in society. Capitalists, trade unions, small businessmen, women, are all to be represented as collectives on the national stage; only the state however, and not the collectives themselves, has the prerogative of choosing who will be the particular representative.

Monetarism or 'libertarianism' on the other hand is a classic form of *laissez-faire*, leaving economic control to the whim of international market forces, and thus generating the purest form of 'open economy' in each nation state. It marks a return to individualism in its crudest form. Collectivities should not exist; there should be only a series of individuals, all equally consumers and all equal before the law, kept from impinging on one another's total freedom by a state which holds no brief for any one individual as against another.

Fascism became an important ideology in Latin America after the collapse of world trade and the old, 'open economies' of the continent in the wake of the Great Depression. Export markets were crumbling, and countries could no longer rely on the proceeds of the sale of primary products to the developed world to finance the import of manufactured goods. Debts contracted on world financial markets had to go by default. It was a situation which prompted the collapse of more than one civilian government, and very often left military men in control or close to the levers of power in emergency governments. State intervention in the economy was unavoidable, and the *laissez-faire* ideologies to which Latin American governments had been committed for several generations seemed wholly inappropriate.

15

Birds of a feather

'There's a good deal of similarity between the economic policies of Chile and those of Great Britain.'

Cecil Parkinson, Tory Minister of Trade, Santiago, October 1980.

JENNY MATTHEWS/FORMAT

During the interview he showed a lively interest in the Chilean economic experience, which, he said, 'is very similar to what we are trying to develop now in Great Britain'.

'What aspects of the two economic policies do you find so similar?'

'Well, for instance, we don't believe in high tariffs and we're trying to reduce them. We want to cut state expenditure, the state bureaucracy, and taxes on profits. We're removing controls and restrictions on prices, wages, the exchange rate and investment overseas. We want to break up the monopoly of nationalized enterprises, selling some to the private sector and opening up others in competition. As you can see, it's a situation very like the one which faced the Chilean economy. At bottom, we feel it is necessary to cut the role of the public sector and re-establish the role of the private sector.'

'And what would you see as the chief differences between the two experiences?'

'The basic difference is that our experience takes place in a democratic context, and that of Chile was undertaken by an authoritarian regime. So Chile could impose a policy and a speed of application in that policy which just isn't possible in this country. Here we have to work with the consent of the majority, so we have to proceed more cautiously and convince people of the benefits of this policy.'

'And do you think this situation poses any threat to the economic programme of your government? Can it demonstrate its benefits before the next general election?'

'When we won the election a year and a half ago, people knew our programme and knew it would be tough. We didn't hide the fact that there will be unemployment and economic difficulties, but we still got a large majority. We believe that we won't lose that majority over the next few months, so we aren't afraid of failing to·carry our programme through to its conclusion. We think that in two or three years, the new way of things will show its advantages. Unemployment will fall, the economy will grow and inflation will fall still further than it has done already, since it has fallen this year from 22 per cent to 16 per cent. Once inflation comes down, interest rates will fall and our exports will become more competitive. So we aren't afraid that Britain will leave the path of virtue after the next elections.'

El Mercurio Weekly Report
October 1980

Military men at the time were very conscious of the importance of a local armaments industry to back up a modern war, and had already taken steps to establish this kind of industry in countries such as Chile and Argentina. They were sympathetic to the proposition that the state should take an active part in any programme of national industrialization, particularly if it could do so in a fashion which kept Latin America's revolutionary anarcho-syndicalist or communist labour movements under firm control.

The influence of fascist ideologies in one Latin American country after another during this period has been a well-kept secret. After the Allied victory against the Axis, which had provided the model for this new form of social experiment, Latin America had to turn to overtly democratic forms of organization, although inconvenient fascist sympathies in some trustworthy authoritarian allies of the United States were simply 'overlooked'; Somoza in Nicaragua is a good example.

Fascism was able to put on patriotic dress in Latin America in the 1930s because it *was* a form of economic nationalism, advocating that governments impose a strict political control on all international economic ties. It suited the needs of those sectors of society who would benefit most from a project of industrialization, notably the military and the local industrial elites. It did a great deal in its time to fashion the basic institutional framework of the emerging industrial societies (labour legislation being one notable example). It also pioneered a range of economic measures, from complicated exchange rates to the foundation of national steel and petroleum industries aimed at generating industrial growth. All these measures have been subsequently condemned by the new ideologists of 'libertarianism' as forms of monopoly likely to encourage a lazy and inefficient managerial elite.

Fascist ideologies thus have deep roots even in a country like Chile, where the original experiment was premature and largely unsuccessful. Subsequently, explicitly fascist economic theories were displayed almost everywhere in Latin America, even by the democratic economic nationalism of such bodies as the United Nations Economic Commission for Latin America (ECLA) which reflected a world where government intervention in economic affairs had been legitimized by Keynes.

Bland monetarism

The new monetarist creed is a different creature entirely. It combines its primary belief in the sanctity of free market forces with an effective *internationalism* in economic affairs. This implies that nations should not try to hold on to industries which are not profitable within the framework of an integrated world economy, however strategically vital they may be. It is an appropriate ideology for a world where multinational corporations have become the norm. Perhaps it is also an appropriate ideology for a world where local businessmen in many countries themselves prefer to take their profits and bank them in Miami, or invest in Californian real estate.

In most South American countries where advocates of these ideas have found a sympathetic hearing with the new authoritarian governments of the 1960s and 1970s, they have faced considerable opposition from the old military establishment. Yet this is the very force on which their quest for power ultimately depends, and created the state sector which the new technocrats propose to demolish. The old military establishments tend to have visions of the future in which the nation is an economic as well as a political Great Power. They may not be fascists — the more common word for them in Latin America now is nationalists — but they do represent a kind of naturalized local variant of the fascist tradition. Like the fascists, they tend to be specialists in applying violence to the body politic, which gives them a certain weight of their own in local political affairs within an authoritarian regime. As exiles from the new military dictatorship in Brazil were saying in Chile in the early 1970s: 'The liberals in our government are the pro-Americans; it is our torturers who are the anti-imperialists.'

When the history of South America's dictatorships during this period is written, the tug-of-war between *blandos* or *laissez-faire* authoritarian liberals and *duros* or authoritarian nationalists will surely emerge as one of its consistent features. In most of the new authoritarian governments, the *blandos* have had to rely on the *duros* to carry out the systematic repression which their policies required. They have therefore not had it all their own way. In Argentina for example, until the invasion of the Malvinas/Falklands in 1982, it was a case of the Emperor Who Had No Clothes. Monetarists were able to use the power of the state to force down wages, but opposition within the armed forces kept them from raising the level of unemployment to the point where market forces would keep wages down 'naturally'. In addition, the state's holdings in industry were virtually untouchable. The invasion of the Malvinas/Falklands seems to have been designed as a sop to the nationalists while a new minister of the economy set out more determinedly on the classic orthodox *laissez-faire* road. But it failed, and so did he.

Only in Chile has there been a 'pure' monetarist experiment over

Fascism and corporatism in Chile

Fascist ideas first made their appearance in Chile during the military dictatorship of Carlos Ibañez (1926-1931), a contemporary and admirer of Mussolini. It was an era when Chile's political parties had demonstrably failed to cope with economic crisis, contributing to widespread disillusionment with democratic leaders. The rejection of Chile's well-established and deeply-rooted political parties has been the hallmark of Chile's fascist and authoritarian movements ever since. It was also during the Ibañez era that such groups adopted Diego Portales, the dictator who created Chile's first stable national government, as their hero and ideological trademark — with some encouragement from Augustin Edwards, then director of *El Mercurio*. It is no accident today that Pinochet's seat of government is named 'Diego Portales'.

Ibañez was the first president of Chile to set about deliberately encouraging local industrialization as a way of cutting back on imports, and many of the reforms he introduced were geared to this aim. But the immediate attraction of Mussolini's ideas in Chile, where workers were organized through strong unions with anarcho-syndicalist or socialist loyalties, was the promise they held out of a solution to the social question which went beyond mere repression. The ministry of labour discussed Italy's 'corporations', and Mussolini's *Carta de Lavoro* was aired in *El Mercurio*, with contributions from prominent church figures such as Fr. Viviani, leader of the church's own union movement.

Nevertheless, as a dictator, Ibañez himself had no immediate need for the kind of mobilization politics which fascism implied. He was supported by the Germanic traditions of total obedience in his own army — like Pinochet himself fifty years later. These ideas took root as a social phenomenon when Ibañez fell from power as the result of a second economic collapse due to the Great Depression. From exile, he supported any movement which looked likely to bring him back to power by electoral means or the force of arms. Thus, during the 1930s, Chile developed a series of small fascist political parties, among them a German-style Nationalist Party which was able to muster support particularly among the German farming communities in the south. As a political force, these were never much more than fringe groups trying to rival Chile's more conventional parties of the right and left, but they did successfully organize mass demonstrations and secured the tacit support of some officers on active service.

The 1930s movement collapsed when the young nazis attempted to assassinate President Alessandri, the conservative elected to power in

♦

1932. The outcome was a massacre of the would-be assassins and the end of fascism as a mass political movement.

More respectable figures in Chile's catholic and business community were also flirting with corporatist ideas during the 1930s, particularly through the journal *Estudios*. Antipathetic to the old political system based on parties, this periodical offered instead one essentially based on *gremios*, whether those of employers, professionals, or workers. It was an idea which attracted support from the organization of large landowners (SNA), and the most important business confederation, the Confederation of Production and Commerce. This kind of businessman's corporatism favoured an authoritarian order where control would rest effectively with the *gremios*, without the inconvenience of a führer or a fascist party. It was very much the tradition upon which *El Mercurio* drew during the campaign against Allende — not surprisingly, perhaps, as its sub-editor Arturo Fontaine was educated in the *Estudios* tradition. From this tradition springs the formula as to the importance of *intermediate* organizations between the state and civil society, always referred to in the official documents of the Pinochet regime.

Fascism of a purer kind also survived, to swell the broad campaign which re-elected Ibañez as President in 1952 on a platform expressing disillusion with the political parties and promising a 'new broom'. However, Ibañez did very little to alter Chile's existing democratic system during his period of office (although he did leave the legacy of a tough Law for the Defence of the Security of State, much drawn on by the present government). Disillusioned by his apparent conversion to the old system, Chile's fascists began to emerge in modern form as tiny sects, largely without popular support, basing their hopes on possible sympathy for their cause within the armed forces. One group however, the *Linea Recta*, is supposed to have been formed within the military establishment itself.

These were the seeds which blossomed during Allende's presidency into the practitioners of street violence and became the source of the most obvious civilian challenge to the government (and possibly military challenge as well). They were never quite as significant as they looked to their opponents, but their ideas do seem to have had an indirect impact on the officer corps. One such group, Fatherland and Freedom *(Patria y Libertad)*, also acquired a mass following among the golden youth of the upper and middle classes.

After the coup, Fatherland and Freedom dissolved itself in a gesture of nationalist abnegation. Other small sects were to survive by making themselves useful to the military in power, staffing its national communications network, (DINACOS), and its trade union desk, the *Secretario de los Gremios*, as well as the secret police, (DINA).

any length of time. The relative willingness of the Chilean government to take such radical steps may well reflect the close call that Chile's business classes had with a possible social revolution. But it may also reflect the relative weakness of corporatist and fascist traditions within Chilean society at large and more particularly within its armed forces. Chile's initial experiments with corporatist ideas came very early, in the 1920s, and was based on the somewhat inconsistent model of Mussolini's Italy. (See Box Page 20). It also ended very early, in 1931, when the military were swept from power in the wake of the Great Depression. Their comparative failure in political and economic affairs kept them out of power for 40 years, and explains more than any other single factor the years of socialist government under President Allende before *El Mercurio's* efforts to produce a military coup bore fruit.

In Chile, the credit for a conscious policy of industrialization is normally given not to the military dictator Ibañez but to a coalition of parties elected to power in an ordinary democratic contest, the 1938 Popular Front, which included communists and socialists as well as radicals. Thus, state intervention in the Chilean economy was promoted by the parties of organized labour, together with the middle class. Popular Unity's programme in 1973 was above all an attempt to build on that conscious effort by labour to direct national economic development in a way that seemed to serve the interests of the majority of the population. It is no accident that Salvador Allende was a minister in that earlier government.

Once Popular Unity had been eliminated, and with it the democratic system which was Chile's most consistent political tradition, the new ideologists of the right faced little significant opposition from the left to their proposals for a drastic economic and social revolution.

3 Popular Unity 1970-1973

The Allende Years

In retrospect, Allende's government seems a last-ditch attempt to defend the national character of the local economy by reaffirming the fundamental right of governments and electors to organize their economic affairs to suit themselves. Such a proposition does not square with the abstract dictates of an international economy.

His government's crucial aim was to restructure Chilean industry, not to make it competitive on international markets as the Chicago Boys would later try to do, but to ensure that it met the basic needs of the population, particularly the poor. Chile's existing industrial capacity was much less sensitive to their needs than to the more sophisticated 'needs' of the wealthy middle classes. They demanded as much variety as possible, and goods such as they could buy in New York or Paris. In market terms, the middle classes had a more powerful vote than workers or peasants, or urban slum-dwellers. Chile's industrialization process had responded quite efficiently to this basic economic fact of life, though its middle class consumers paid a high price for the end product. Thus no fewer than twelve small multinational subsidiaries operated in the field of car production with massive over-capacity, to produce a passable imitation of the range of brand products open to US consumers. Meanwhile, it required state intervention under both the Frei and Allende governments to develop such basic resources as Chile's fisheries and forestry, and without the intervention of the National Development Agency (CORFO), there would have been no fish-processing plants at all.

Chile's existing industry had become more and more integrated into an international pattern — in the kinds of goods it produced, the equipment it produced them with, the advertising which was used to sell them, and the presence of foreign companies as its stockholders. Part of the country's economic problems stemmed from the financial strain which these developments put on the national economy. Instead of saving foreign exchange by substituting locally produced goods for imports, it was actually paying out increasing amounts to finance the import of parts to keep the new machinery going, or to buy new machinery made in the United States to replace the old. All these costs were effectively paid for by copper, whose price fluctuated drastically on international markets — a hazard over which local governments had no control at all. It is no wonder that Popular Unity was to become one of the prime original movers demanding guaranteed prices for the Third World's primary products at the third conference of UNCTAD held in 1973.

But part of the strain was social. The local economy could not use the kind of industry it was importing to provide a sufficient number of jobs to keep its population employed. Yet it still found itself importing a package from the developed countries which reproduced their patterns of consumption and in which mass consumer advertising was as important a part of the package as the type of production. The practical result was that its middle class elite could be 'Western', 'participating' in the new social order as church and Christian Democrat ideology put it so vividly, but its masses were doomed to be forever on the outside looking in. Slum-dwellers, 'marginals' who cannot find work in modern industry, are not a great potential market for cars.

Nothing in this historical experience was particularly unique to Chile. On the contrary, other Latin American countries were also suffering from the same strains. In Brazil, the outcome was a coup in 1964 which deliberately set about concentrating income in the hands of the upper middle class car buyers, at the expense of the poor and urban workers, broadening an already extensive local market for the kind of goods which the new industry could produce superbly.

Popular Unity was to try a different approach, one of reordering the economy to meet the needs of the people, rather than putting the people on a Procrustean bed to meet the needs of the new economic forces.

Initially, its strategy was three-pronged. One of the new government's major commitments was to carry out to the letter the existing Christian Democratic legislation on agrarian reform. This was done for much the same reasons that had originally motivated the Christian Democrats. The government was faced with one of the most serious bottlenecks in the post 1930 economy, the failure to produce

24

enough basic food for the population. A solution was sought through taking land away from the large landowners or *latifundistas* and giving it to the peasants for them to produce food for local consumption. This, it was thought, would both relieve rural poverty and increase demand for industrial products among the newly landed peasantry. The man in charge of the Christian Democrats' own agrarian reform, Jacques Chonchol, crossed over to the new government to administer the programme.

Meanwhile, in the urban areas, the government was also making an effort to give the poor an economic vote. The plan was to reflate the economy by means of the government promotion of construction and other devices such as raising workers' wages. The government's intention was to combine such measures with strict price controls in order to effect a redistribution of income downwards — and also, in the best Keynesian fashion, to motivate industrialists to produce more for the growing new market of the poor in order to lessen the squeeze on their profits.

At the same time, direct control over certain areas of the economy was required to ensure that the restructuring process went ahead. High on the list of priorities were the country's basic resources, such as copper, coal, and iron. But the textile and consumer durable industries and the infant electronics industry (then in private hands) had to be nationalized to provide the kind of goods which Popular Unity wanted. 'People's television sets' and 'people's fridges', basic, mass-produced, and relatively cheap, were part of the new consumer model for the poor which the government was promoting. It was hoped that a vast expansion in their markets would give these industries a greater economic dynamism, and in this way stimulate the economy as a whole. Popular Unity's socialism was not intended to be puritanical; it was intended to reproduce a locally sustainable version of the mass consumer society of the West, with a mixed economy, using mass production techniques to manufacture goods at a price which ordinary local consumers could afford.

Initially, the programme of nationalization was expected to extend to 253 'monopolies'. A year into the government's life, the number involved was cut to 91.

Enemies at Home and Abroad

It is difficult to assess whether this programme could have worked as an economic model if for example the price of copper on world markets had remained high throughout Allende's period in office, and there had been no US blockade of external aid and credits. Without a fully-fledged New International Economic Order, it would still have left the Chilean economy vulnerable to periodic external shocks to its supply lifelines for parts and other crucial equipment. But the question is hardly relevant; in the real world, economics does not exist in isolation from politics, and economic models are rarely judged successful unless they meet the needs of those with most economic power. Popular Unity's attempt to redesign the economic structure which the Chilean population had inherited offended all those, locally and internationally, who had the most power to destroy it.

Local industrialists who faced no direct threat of nationalization themselves were still horrified at the threat to the private sector which such a wholesale range of nationalizations implied. Their instincts were not to preserve short-term profits by expanding production to meet the new demand, but to improve their own long-term profits as a social class by joining the campaign to bring down the government. Well-advertised shortages of supply in essential goods were a critical part of this campaign.

In the real political world, such men had an extremely powerful ally in the US government, which not only cut off Chile's existing commercial credits, but flooded the country with money to aid the opposition. The United States, of course, is bitterly opposed to any form of Marxist government, whether democratically elected or not, and is notoriously unwilling to allow any such government to operate within its sphere of influence. But it was also offended by the treatment which Popular Unity meted out to its multinational copper companies, Anaconda and Kennecott, still owners of 49 per cent of Chile's copper mines after the 'Chileanization' programme of the Christian Democrats. Popular Unity had ostentatiously offered to pay full compensation for the book value of the assets, and then deducted from that sum all profit remittances in excess of 12 per cent return on capital per year made during the previous 15 years. This calculation left both corporations in debt to the Chilean government for millions of dollars.

President Frei's government had not met such hostility from the United States. Not only was it profoundly anti-communist, but it overpaid these same multinational copper companies for the 51 per cent stake in Chile's copper which it bought back from them, whilst leaving them in managerial control. All opposition parties voted with Popular Unity in congress to support the Allende government's nationalization bill. They did not however decline US government financial aid in the campaign to bring Allende's government down.

The opposition also had powerful local allies. Christian Democracy had an extremely well-organized political machine as a result of its work in urban and rural areas over a ten-year period. Workers throughout Chile were thus confronted with an opposition programme at their place of work, offering 'real workers' control' (cooperatives) as an alternative to state management, and picking up quickly any weaknesses in the new government's policies of worker participation. Over a three-year period, such activities had a real impact in only a few places: in the docks of the southern city of Concepción, where docker Eduardo Rios was a Christian Democrat senator, and among white-collar workers in one of the copper mines, *El Teniente*. In many more places workers slowly concluded, whether they were Christian Democrats or not, that their interests were not likely to be served by the violent removal of Allende by a new right wing. In some of the textile factories in Santiago, Christian Democrats and Popular Unity were to join forces to defend the government. In other areas, like the Chuquicamata copper mine in the far north, where Christian Democrats had been elected as representatives, a sense of hopelessness at the scale of the impending tragedy took over.

Not all Christian Democrats were as close to the nerve of what was happening as their trade unionists. Some party members, even among the poor, were worried by the supposed threat of atheism and 'totalitarianism' which a Marxist government might bring. They launched a campaign to preserve private and religious education and to block Popular Unity's modest proposals to introduce comprehensive schools in the name of freedom of education. This drew open support from religious figures, army generals, and many housewives. Old women from the country's urban slums were often to be found on opposition demonstrations.

How Not to Win Friends

Those peasants who had benefited from the original Christian Democrat reform programme were also dissatisfied. The Christian Democrat programme had aimed to turn confiscated *latifundio* land initially into cooperatives for the permanent employees, and subsequently into small private holdings which the members of the cooperative could divide among themselves or farm together, as they preferred. By the time Popular Unity came to power it was clear that such a system would once again divide the rural areas into privileged classes and non-privileged, leaving the younger sons of families with no land of their own and huge numbers of casual labourers or *afuerinos* even more marginalized. Popular Unity proposed instead to use some of the confiscated land to create state farms in which all the agricultural workers were employees. This alienated the smallholders who had looked forward to having their own private

27

property for the first time, and many joined the opposition. They were joined by the German farmers of the south, small capitalists with their own authoritarian traditions.

The economic programme also antagonized powerful sectors in the urban community. Small businessmen, in Popular Unity's view, were frequently exploited by the big monopolists who took components or services from them at a price which swelled monopoly profits. But the small businessmen felt that a massive programme of nationalization threatened private enterprise as such and their own freedom to expand. The right was able to play on fears that nationalization could include everything, from the local newspaper-seller's kiosk on the corner upwards. Such fears were fuelled by the attitudes of workers in small businesses, many of them among the worst paid and most exploited in the country, who sometimes felt that a strike or occupation to force the government to nationalize *their* firms was a way to improve their conditions. As their confidence grew, so too did their willingness to take on their own bosses, by calling on the government to intervene.

Retailers and wholesalers were hostile to the government's attempts to control distribution directly in order to pre-empt the black market. The government set up local supply committees in every working class suburb and gave them direct control over the allocation of goods. Small businessmen saw these measures as a threat to their own freedom to make profit and run their affairs as they wished.

The government programme was equally unacceptable to middle class consumers, particularly women. Increased popular demand meant that some shortages were inevitable, particularly of beef, which was a staple for upper middle class households and the first luxury of choice for most of Chile's poor. Hoarding of goods in the face of price controls and a rapid inflationary process also contributed to a sense of perpetual, arbitrary shortages: first tins of tomatoes, then teats for baby bottles, then perhaps toilet paper, or cigarettes. Meanwhile, the papers controlled by the left and its single television channel were full of pictures of urban slum-dwellers with new television sets.

These were the roots out of which the opposition constructed the *gremio* movement: an ill-assorted ragbag of professional associations of doctors and lawyers, businessmen's associations, farmers' organizations and 'the women of Chile' (as *El Mercurio* called them), in other words middle class housewives. It was a movement representing everything from the owner of a great landed estate to the peasant farmer defending the plot of land he hoped for as a result of agrarian reform. Very little held the movement together except the shared indignation towards the incumbent government, whipped up to a fury by *El Mercurio*.

Popular Unity was well aware of its own critical need to win over as many as possible of the middle sectors, and spent three years in power arguing about the best way to do so. The Communist Party called for permanent negotiations with the Christian Democrats. The left in the Popular Unity coalition hoped that a determined thrust towards change would in the end carry the bulk of these sectors along with it. Time was to prove both arguments over-optimistic.

4 The Making of the Coup 1970-1973

Who Planned the Coup?

It is all too easy to see the coup of 11 September 1973 as the product of a Machiavellian conspiracy directed by the CIA, ex-President Frei, or, if we are to believe his autobiography, personally planned, timetabled and carried out by General Pinochet.

The truth is that responsibility cannot be pinned down so easily. Ultimately, it lies not with any small set of conspirators, but with the half of the Chilean population who joined opposition demonstrations over a period of three years and played their part in supporting the web of reaction and counter-reaction which enmeshed Allende's government. These were the people who chose Frei's 'Revolution in Liberty' in 1964. By 1973, for whatever reasons of personal self-interest or anti-Soviet hysteria, confusion and illusion, they were prepared to replace it with counter-revolution and tyranny. Not necessarily a conscious choice, but an effective one all the same.

Nevertheless, coups do require a tremendous amount of organization and planning. It is worth studying how this one was made, because it shows the role of human action in politics, and because it allows us to understand many of the developments which followed in October 1973.

The Americans Try and Fail and Try Again

Both the Chilean right and the United States were caught off-balance by Allende's victory. Edward Korry, the US Ambassador in Chile, had been so confident of a right-wing Alessandri victory that he had not even set up any coordinating machinery in case of a victory for the left. The US State Department quickly gave Korry 'maximum authority to do all possible, short of a Dominican Republic-type action, to keep Allende from taking power'. (In 1965, 20,000 marines invaded the Dominican Republic). But as the memos from the US transnational company ITT reveal, local moves to prevent Allende assuming the presidency were badly coordinated and even worse executed. Allende had been elected in the normal democratic fashion, and although there were both Chilean and American conspirators, they were initially operating without any real support from the Chilean population.

The immediate reaction of the Chilean rich was to get their money out of Chile. In many cases, they left with it. Those who stayed favoured a constitutional ruse to prevent Allende taking over the presidency. Legally, the president of Chile had to be ratified by congress after his election by a popular vote. Alessandri's supporters proposed that they and the Christian Democrats vote together against Allende's ratification, given that they still controlled the majority of the seats in congress. Thereafter, Alessandri would be declared president, would call elections, and would then stand down in favour of President Frei, who was constitutionally debarred from standing for a second term of office when he had just completed his first. Frei however refused to comply, much to the fury of ITT and the US embassy. Accusations and counter-accusations over this incident were to resurface after the coup, when the right blamed Frei for the three years of socialist government.

After the failure of this manoeuvre, a group of extreme right-wing conspirators gathered round General Viaux (leader of an open army mutiny against Frei). Their plan, supported by the CIA, was to fake a 'left-wing kidnapping' of the head of the Chilean armed forces, General Schneider, with the objective of creating panic in the armed forces and provoking a coup. But the kidnap attempt was badly bungled, and Schneider himself died in the shooting. Schneider had favoured keeping the army out of politics; the manner of his death enabled other constitutionalists within its ranks to make it impossible for any army officer to advocate getting rid of Allende before he took power.

A third tactic was favoured by Radomiro Tomic, a Christian Democrat candidate in the 1970 elections, and leader of a generally left-wing faction of the party. The Christian Democrats would agree to ratify Allende's election in congress in return for his signature on a Statute of Guarantees, in which he would promise to uphold the constitution and the legal system. It was an attempt to ensure that Allende maintained the existing constitutional arrangements so that Popular Unity's real legislative programme could only be mildly reformist because of having to take into account the opposition majority in congress. Allende signed.

Much to the fury of ITT, the United States was forced to accept Allende's accession to power. The company's executives huffed:

'Why should the United States try to be so pious and sanctimonious in September and October, when over the past few years it has been pouring the taxpayers' money into Chile, specifically to defeat Marxism? Why can't the fight be continued now, now that the battle is in the home stretch and the enemy more clearly identifiable?'

They need not have worried. The Nixon administration was already putting together a plan to destabilize the Chilean government. After the initial confusion, a consensus had emerged between Ambassador Korry, the CIA, ITT, and Kissinger, that Popular Unity's weak point was the economy. Over the next three years, that weakness would be systematically exacerbated by a deliberate US attempt to cut the international supply lines to local industry, depriving them of vital parts for their machines by suspending all American suppliers' credits and trying to upset their commercial relations with other Western sources. Meanwhile, if money and assistance could sustain the opposition, then over time that opposition could organize a mass movement of protest and create such a sense of chaos that the armed forces would be forced to intervene. Two problems remained: the armed forces themselves, and the nature of the Chilean opposition.

Reluctant Soldiers

Most of the Chilean officer corps was solidly anti-communist. President Frei had introduced the practice of sending many of them on special anti-subversion courses run by the US military. Normal joint programmes between the US and Chilean military establishments were maintained throughout the Popular Unity period. So too was US financial assistance for military programmes, which actually grew during the Allende years while all other US aid was being suspended.

Nevertheless, those organizing the coup found it difficult to get sufficient support within the military while it was committed to Schneider's brand of constitutionalism and the economic nationalism and developmentalism he had also supported. Schneider's successor, Carlos Prats, offered them similar problems. The Chilean right accordingly regarded the armed forces as hopelessly backward in political terms. As one leading figure in the preparations for the coup put it:

'The civilians made the coup. Our problem was how to get the armed forces to execute it. The problem was that the Chilean armed forces were very backward politically (no other armed forces in Latin America would have allowed Allende to last three years) and it required a mass civilian movement to get the armed forces to act.'

From Congress to the Press

The initial fragmentation of the Chilean opposition in the face of Allende's victory was more easily solved. Shortly after the election, Frei regained control of the Christian Democrats from his own left-wing, and in June 1971 the Christian Democrat Party and National Party signed a pact committing them both to oppose Popular Unity. Effectively, Allende now faced a hostile majority in both congress and senate. Through the impeachment of his ministers, and by blocking his legislation and proposing their own alternative plans, the opposition planned to destroy Allende's ability to govern.

In the event, they were unsuccessful. Allende and his ministers proved adept at side stepping and by passing the legislature. Takeovers of local industry, which should have been illegal under the legislation passed by the opposition majority, were legitimized by resurrecting a little-known law from the 1932 Socialist Republic, which allowed governments to intervene in any industry where management was failing to maintain production. Slowly but inevitably, the struggle emerged from the halls of congress and onto the streets. But the impression created by congressmen, senators and judges that Allende's government was 'constitutionally illegal' was enormously useful to the opposition in legitimizing its own activities.

The three daily newspapers owned by the Edwards family, *La Segundo, Las Ultimas Noticias,* and *El Mercurio,* took advantage of these developments to mount a massive and, in retrospect, wholly cynical campaign in defence of democracy. Every act of Popular Unity was presented as an erosion of fundamental rights and democratic principles, a threat to the rule of law, and a danger to the very basis of the Christian and Western values which Chile was meant to embody. A proposal to associate the faculty of law with the faculty of social sciences in Chile's state university, for instance, was greeted as 'a harbinger of the decline in the role of law in Western civilization'. Reforms which Popular Unity introduced with the intention of extending democratic participation had constantly to be defended on the grounds that they did not endanger 'democracy' itself.

As the economy ran into problems, and the opposition's propaganda campaign grew more clamorous, the majority of Chile's middle classes began to believe that the defence of wealth, privilege and economic power were one and the same as the defence of their household property and the democratic system. Rather than dividing the tiny monopoly sector from the rest of the Chilean population as it had hoped, Popular Unity suffered the effects of a spectacular surge of popular mobilization in defence of that minority. More than a press campaign was needed — nothing less than a shift in the traditional style of right-wing politics and the personal ethos of its politicians was essential. The strategy was brilliantly summed up by *El Mercurio* itself:

'However the opposition organizes itself, its methods of action must have an immediate root in the bases of society: it cannot confine itself to the general propaganda and traditional use of assemblies by the old political parties. Neighbourhood councils, mothers' unions, cooperatives, trade unions and other professional bodies require the permanent involvement of those representing the best political thinking of the citizens: not the reduced contacts characteristic of an electoral campaign. The explicit or implicit unity of the opposition should give rise to concrete actions at work, in the suburb, in the supermarket, which will be capable of counteracting the dictatorship which the Marxists are prepared to put into practice at the base. It is not enough for the democratic forces to try to reach the public through the mass media. They must link themselves with the masses. Such a programme implies great sacrifice, often a substantial change of people's habits and style of life.'

In mid 1971, a group of influential figures without strong party ties began to meet on a regular basis to coordinate the burgeoning campaign against Allende. One of their members called them 'the Monday Club' because they met every Monday for lunch in the offices of Hernan Cubillos, in Lord Cochrane Street. Cubillos had been left in charge of the Edwards' business empire when Doonie Edwards fled the country, and one of his most important responsibilities was *El Mercurio*. He was also widely assumed to be one of the CIA's key contacts in Chile.

The main participants in this group were Cubillos himself, up-and-coming businessman Javier Vial; another businessman with close family ties with the Edwards empire, Jorge Ross; the head of the association of Chilean manufacturers, Orlando Saenz; and the editor of *El Mercurio*, Raul Silva Espejo. They were joined on occasion by *El Mercurio's* sub-editor, Arturo Fontaine, who was later to take over the editorship from Raul Silva. Two other critically important figures in the network of the 'Chicago Boys' were linked with the group: Emilio Sanfuentes, an economist trained in Chicago and owner of *Que Pasa* (a weekly magazine set up to raise middle class support for *laissez-faire* economics); and Manuel Cruzat, another highly ambitious Chicago graduate. Cruzat and Vial were both to make their fortunes out of the privatization of state industries following the coup.

This group seems to have been one of the main channels for money coming from private firms in Venezuela, Mexico, and elsewhere, into Chile to finance the opposition to Allende. Much of this was a cover for funds coming directly from the CIA.

Besides its role as surrogate banker, the Monday Club offered the *gremio* movement leadership and coordination. Like all semi-spontaneous mass movements, the *gremios* had strong anarchistic tendencies. The leadership of this supposedly 'apolitical' movement devolved naturally on the shoulders of the editor and proprietor of *El Mercurio*, the voice of 'reasoned public opinion'. The preservation of its apolitical dimension was critical for all the parties concerned; for the Monday Club, the *gremios*, and *El Mercurio* itself. By claiming to be 'non-political' in a highly politicized environment, the *gremios* could cut right across party political barriers and the sectarian divisions which were a traditional feature of Chilean life. They could gather behind them people who might otherwise have been distinctly wary of taking to the streets in such unsavoury company. They could also appeal directly to the armed forces, 'non-political' and ostensibly constitutionalist themselves, in the name of the people of Chile. Thus it was a distinct advantage for both the Monday Club and *El Mercurio* to maintain their distance from Chile's traditional political parties, even those which were organizing the opposition campaign in congress.

As for the opposition Nationalist and Christian Democrat parties, their attitude to the emergence of these new right-wing forces varied. The National Party was content to operate almost wholly within the *gremio* movement, keeping its overtly 'political' activities solely for congress. For nationalists, it was more important to ensure the survival of the capitalist system than it was to ensure their own survival as a political entity. For the Christian Democrats, the *gremios* presented a more complex problem. The corporatist strand in their ideology was part and parcel of Christian Democracy's own heritage. But as a multi-class coalition led by professional politicians, Christian Democrats had a deep interest in preserving their own distinctive identity as a party, and were unwilling to dissolve that identity inside another political movement. They therefore never gave unreserved support to the *gremios*.

The *gremio* movement encouraged a brief resurgence of the old corporatist and authoritarian motif in Chilean political thought, a hatred of politicians and hatred of the political parties who were 'ruining the country'. Raul Silva Espejo himself belonged to that tradition, and he was able to give it voice and direction through *El Mercurio*. Another important figure in articulating the *gremios'* ideas was a fanatical young lawyer at the Catholic University, Jaime Guzman, and his acolytes in the Catholic University student federation.

This authentically corporatist movement mingled with the old fascists of Chile and some new ones, coming from a patchwork of different groups with Spanish, German and other loyalties. The most sinister and effective of these groups was Fatherland and Freedom, led by a man who seemed to see himself as a possible new führer, Pablo Rodriguez Grez. Throughout the Popular Unity period, his members hovered on the fringe of the strikes and demonstrations of the right, ready to foment trouble through assassinations and bombings, and looking for sympathizers within the armed forces. Other groups had a more limited role. Dr Alvayay and some of his sympathizers in the medical profession in Valparaiso manipulated Chilean doctors into supporting the *gremio* movement. A tiny francoist fragment modelling itself on the Spanish ideologue Ledesma and his Workers National Union Committee (JONS) played a role in dividing Valparaiso's trade union movement.

Like the corporatists, Chile's fascists made a virtue of their distrust of parties and politicians. Their distinctive contribution was to carry such distrust to its logical conclusion: a total and open denunciation of the very framework of liberal democracy itself and a desire to replace it with a system in which the state had total authority.

However, the main leaders of the *gremio* movement were not ideologues. Men such as Leon Villarin, ex-socialist, leader of the truck drivers' union, and Rafael Cumsille, leader of the retailers' association, were popular with their members and responsive to their complaints. Villarin, a man easily flattered by association with the rich and powerful, was skilfully manipulated by the Monday Club, only to be dropped immediately after the coup. So indeed was Pablo Rodriguez.

A different phenomenon entirely were the 'women of Chile'. Their core was a well-organized nucleus of the wives of leading opposition politicians, dominated by the National Party. Their inspiration seems to have come from a female journalist at *El Mercurio*, who had attempted to organize a demonstration of women outside the presidential palace as Allende took power, but could only find five supporters. The media played on the irritation felt by middle class housewives at some real scarcities, and their enormous anger at finding their class in competition for food and other essential goods with the Workers' Supply Committees. It was these women who took part in the first mass demonstration which the opposition organized in December 1971, known as the March of the Empty Pots.

This group's most significant contribution to the coup was its success in organizing a vicious campaign of psychological pressure on the armed forces, in the name of 'the women of Chile'. Letters were sent to Leigh, Merino, Pinochet, and other prominent generals of the period questioning their virility and pleading that they 'save our families' from the chaos and violence being perpetrated by Popular Unity. White feathers were sent to all the officer corps as a token of their 'cowardice' in failing to overthrow the civilian government, and wheat was thrown into barracks, implying that the soldiers were 'chickens'. The pressure reached its height in the weeks before the coup, and was one of the significant factors in forcing Prats' resignation, and the end of 'constitutionalism' as an army doctrine.

A myth was thus created: that the country had been saved by 'the women of Chile' demanding that soldiers fulfil their rightful role as protectors of women and families. It was a good media product, which bore little relation to the more sordid reality behind it, that of upper class housewives desperately trying to preserve their level of consumption at the expense of their working class sisters.

Beauty and the Beast: Chicago Meets the Armed Forces

Increasingly throughout 1971 and 1972 the initiatives lay with the right, who appropriated tactics and methods long associated with the left in their struggle to bring down the government. By 1972, plans were in place to bring the country to a standstill through strikes, in the hope of forcing Allende to resign or the armed forces to intervene.

The incident which brought these plans to fruition in October 1972 was a relatively unimportant dispute in Punta Arenas between the private Lorry-Owners' Association and a recently nationalized factory. The association declared a strike in the name of free enterprise and against state interference. Within days, virtually the whole of Chile was paralysed, showing the extraordinary degree of coordination which existed throughout the *gremio* movement. All sectors of the capitalist class staged a lockout; shopkeepers closed their shops, private factories closed their gates, private transport firms locked up their vehicles, and doctors, dentists and lawyers closed their practices. It was the first general strike of the bourgeoisie, and their demands rapidly shifted from the strictly economic to the political, as the movement became a coordinated effort to oust Allende from power.

The right had miscalculated on two fronts: the reaction of Chilean workers, and the reaction of the armed forces. Workers refused to sit idly by while their bosses locked them out. Organizing themselves on a local basis through *cordones* or zone commands, they took the factories, transport and distribution systems into their own hands. The country rapidly reached a stalemate. Allende, desperate to avoid a worse confrontation, appealed to the armed forces for help. General

Prats and two other generals joined the government.

The right were baffled by the Chilean armed forces. They knew through their personal contacts that the vast majority of officers hated Popular Unity. And yet the armed forces refused to intervene, and when they did allow themselves to be drawn in, it was to enforce a state of truce between left and right in a way which infuriated the leaders of the *gremio* movement. Had the right known it, they were looking at an institutional feature of the armed forces which would be of vital importance to the Chicago Boys in years to come.

Chile's military establishment was dominated by the army, and this in turn was governed by a rigid hierarchical structure which made any form of internal debate or political mutiny exceptionally difficult. The head of the army, General Prats, was a constitutionalist, and it would need enormous force to prise his subordinate officers free from their obedience to him. Years of isolation from civilian politics had left the armed forces as a whole unsure as to how to organize and take political decisions. Nevertheless, the assault on this institutional reluctance soon began to make headway, as the navy and the air force took the first steps towards preparations for a coup.

General Prats' intention was to hold the balance between the contending forces until the March 1973 congressional elections, which would offer a chance to test Popular Unity's electoral mandate. In fact, the elections altered nothing. Popular Unity increased its original share of the vote from 37 per cent to 43 per cent, but the opposition retained a clear majority, with 56 per cent. Both sides had won, and the country remained in deadlock.

The Chicago Plan

Contrary to the impression given in General Pinochet's memoirs, it was the naval officers who first decided that the only way to break that deadlock was by seriously preparing a coup to remove Allende from power. The navy, from its Valparaiso base, was in constant telecommunication with the US military, who may have played a part in this decision. But it was also the navy which had closest contacts with the Monday Club. Hernan Cubillos was an ex-naval officer.

The key naval officers in this subversive plot were the captains Troncoso, Castro and Lopez. However, they lacked any idea as to what could be done about the Chilean economy in the immediate aftermath of the coup. They communicated this anxiety to Roberto Kelly, a friend and business associate of Hernan Cubillos, and through Cubillos the message was passed to Orlando Saenz. The outcome was a development which was to provide the Chicago Boys with a natural springboard to power.

Saenz, as president of the Association of Chilean Manufacturers (SOFOFA), had a research department whose head, Sergio Undurraga, was an economist trained at the Catholic University of Santiago. Although not himself a Chicago graduate, Undurraga formed part of the local 'Chicago network', which had already begun to meet informally to discuss the state of the economy. Emilio Sanfuentes and Undurraga now suggested that the meetings be formalized, in order to draw up a plan for the economy in the event of Allende's downfall.

In many ways this was a natural development, and merely demonstrates the wisdom of the original US aid project which set out to establish close ties between the departments of economics at the Catholic University in Chile and the University of Chicago. The Catholic University has a long tradition of educating Chile's right, and the network of those influenced by Chicago ideas was now a very important one. Its links stretched into the main opposition parties, leading business and *gremio* circles, the Monday Club itself and now into the armed forces. It was a socially cohesive network, bound by strong ties of friendship, marriage, and, for most of its members, common life experiences at the department of economics and the University of Chicago. Not everyone from such a background was automatically part of the network however. Rolf Lüders, the man who would become minister of the economy in 1982 when the Chicago model was in ruins, was cordially loathed by the Chicago Boys and never entered the charmed circle.

From March 1973 on, the Chicago Boys began to put together their alternative economic plan in earnest. Facilities and assistance were supplied by SOFOFA as required. The Monday Club was catering in its usually efficient fashion for the organizational needs of a military takeover. Virtually the whole of the Christian Democrat Party's economics department was involved: Alvaro Bardon, Andre Sanfuentes, Jose Luis Zabala and Juan Villarzu. Pablo Baraona provided the direct link with the National Party, and the other five, Sergio de Castro, Manuel Cruzat, Sergio Undurraga (another National Party member), Juan Braun and Emilio Sanfuentes were either leading businessmen in their own right or in close personal contact with these personalities, as well as with the Monday Club itself. Some people were to drop in and out, but the hard core of those involved in drawing up this plan were all to reach prominence after the coup.

Leaders of both the opposition political parties were aware that a plan for Chile's future economy was being drafted. However, it was in their interests to keep such activities unofficial, without any formal backing from headquarters. Nevertheless, the plan bears the hallmarks of a typically negotiated document, above all in the areas on which the Christian Democrats were most sensitive, such as agrarian reform and forms of property ownership.

Even so, most of the key elements in the Chicago model were already present. Above all, the opening up of Chile's local economy to the healthy effects of freer international trade, by reducing tariff barriers and emphasizing export-led growth and production of those goods for which the country had an international comparative advantage, namely those that Chile could produce more cheaply than its international competitors. The commitment to privatization was there, not only for those firms which Popular Unity had nationalized, but for whole areas of the economy where the state had traditionally played a dominant role. There was an obvious distrust of the role of the state in economic matters, particularly its crucial historic role in Chile in providing investment funds and taking investment decisions. The Chicago Boys wanted a strong private capital market.

Perhaps most significant was the strong influence of Hayek on the plan's view of inflation, one of Chile's most persistent historical problems. Inflation was seen as the outcome of strong pressure group influence on a political machine whose rights to intervene in the workings of the economy knew no limits. It represented in effect a collusion between strong trade unions, politicians, and businessmen who had been cushioned by a highly protected economy into thinking that they could live with any economic inputs, however irrational.

As the document was produced, it was systematically leaked to Captain Troncoso by Emilio Sanfuentes. The navy in turn passed it on to trusted generals in the air force. One can doubt whether any of these officers read much of the plan, still less that they understood what it entailed. But the document was important. It created the impression among the armed forces that someone knew how to cope with the economic chaos which would face them as soon as they took over government. In fact, the final version of the plan was ready only days before the coup. Copies were sent to Eduardo Frei and Senator Onofre Jarpa of the National Party, and Orlando Saenz sent a copy to Admiral Merino, while Emilio Sanfuentes sent the final version to Troncoso.

On the military side, events moved fast. The network of military conspirators began to cohere, first in the navy, then in the air force, then between the two. The problem remained the army, without whose support a navy-air force coup would be problematic. Isolated and aloof from his fellow generals, General Prats still commanded respect among the soldiers. To move against him might risk dividing the army, thereby plunging the country into civil war.

In the attempted coup of 29 June 1973 led by Colonel Souper of the tank regiment, inspired and assisted by Fatherland and Freedom, Prats personally took charge of the operation against Souper and quickly crushed the rebellion. General Pinochet was at his side and obeyed Prats' commands with alacrity. Pablo Rodriguez and others fled into embassies, complaining bitterly that certain generals had let them down. However, after 29 June a number of army generals, among them Arellano Stark, Bonilla, Palacios, and Nuño, together with air force generals and naval admirals, sent a memo to Allende with a list of demands. Prats was not consulted. The demands gave no hint of an impending coup or of any non-constitutional action. Nevertheless, the memo represented the most significant move yet towards unity of purpose amongst the chiefs of the three branches of the armed forces.

The civilians kept up their pressure with bombings, assassinations, and another series of mass strikes. The calls for a coup became increasingly vociferous, with *El Mercurio* openly expounding the benefits of a military takeover.

Prats finally succumbed to the pressure. 'To preserve the unity of the army', he offered his resignation as its commander-in-chief. Allende reluctantly agreed, in effect signing his own death warrant. The navy was the first to decide to move. They informed the air force and sympathetic army generals that they would launch the coup with or without the army. The key army generals informed the new head of the armed forces, General Pinochet, that they too would go ahead with or without him. He decided to join them, and subsequently rewrote history with himself as the key figure, in a country where no one would dare to challenge his version of events in public.

Until the last days of Allende, civilian conspirators were unsure of the army. Orlando Saenz, for example, was still anxiously awaiting the message from the army on 9 September. The message, from General Palacios, that 'insulin was needed for his mother', was the signal that the coup was on and the army would take part. Saenz, Kelly and others met the next day in the office of Hugo Leon, a leading construction entrepreneur, to run off copies of the economic plan.

The plan, as Saenz recognized, was unfinished. There had been no agreement on the nature of the subsequent government. The coup was therefore not a structured one. Because of the hierarchical nature of the armed forces, it had been impossible to negotiate any proposals, and thus the economic plan itself had no real status. Their attempt to control history had left the civilian conspirators with an unknown soldier, General Pinochet, in charge.

Nonetheless, as Emilio Sanfuentes was to claim later, 'in a country like Chile, thirty determined persons are unstoppable'. Like the opportunistic Pinochet, the Chicago Boys were on their way to power.

5 The Transition 1973-1974

The Military Emerge From Barracks

The coup began in Valparaiso, the navy's home port. Within 24 hours it was clearly successful. Popular Unity was out of power and its parties were banned. The military themselves had begun the process then called 'cutting out the cancer' and 'cleaning out the stables'. They systematically arrested thousands of suspects and herded them into football stadiums in Santiago and elsewhere. President Allende was dead, killed during the course of an assault on the presidential palace.

A week before the coup, Allende had called in Orlando Saenz and warned him that the future of Chile under a military regime was grim. 'Look at other Latin American countries', he told Saenz. 'It won't be as easy to get the military out of power as it was to tempt them into it, not nearly as easy as getting rid of this government.' (See Box Page 101).

It was a perceptive warning, but Saenz was not prepared to listen. Nor were the opposition parties with whom Allende had already tried negotiating, in the case of the Christian Democrats over many long months. The fact is that Christian Democrat politicians did indeed believe that the military were stepping onto the political scene as emergency caretakers, and would disappear once the job of eliminating an 'unpopular' government was done. The opposition had no serious apprehensions about the role of the military in the future. There were thus no protests from the opposition parties as congress was closed, its elected representatives stripped of their mandate, and their own rights to operate publicly suspended, the country put under a state of siege and media censorship introduced.

Djakarta

When the coup came, *El Mercurio* had already spent months highlighting the virtues of the Indonesian model, where a ruthless military dictatorship aided by US technical assistance had stepped in to suppress the weak populist government of Sukarno, massacre the local communist population and lay the basis for an economic boom. Djakarta, the synonym for massacre, was the emblem which Fatherland and Freedom had scrawled on walls all over Santiago. Like so much else in the new regime, it was an imported model.

Also imported, and explaining much of the violence (which left the Santiago morgue struggling to cope with nearly 3,000 bodies two weeks after the coup) was the doctrine which sent Chile's armed forces to war against its own population. The notion of a war against Popular Unity should have been absurd. Popular Unity had no standing army. Such plans for self-defence as the government parties had made were based on the assumption that the army would split, with one part at least defending the constitutional government. Workers with small arms could then rally to the defence of the republic, as they had in Spain.

Nevertheless, the new doctrine of National Security (See Box Page 44) assiduously promoted by the United States *did* preach war against civilians. It promoted a theory that modern wars were necessarily 'total wars' which involved one side trying to eliminate the other as a physical, social and political force. In such circumstances civilian deaths were no more or less part of war than the deaths of men-at-arms. Torture was a wholly legitimate form of self-defence which could naturally be included in the training courses. Quite apart from its tendency to turn all political tensions into a Holy War against communism, the National Security Doctrine is a terrifying creation. In Chile, it turned the systematic and sadistic use of violence and torture into a pillar of the state.

Such resistance as there was to the coup came from a few snipers on apartment blocks and offices, a few workers who were determined to 'hold' their factories against the tanks at least for a time, and from a myth. The myth was that of Salvador Allende, a consummate politician who had exhausted every form of persuasive argument, compromise, political manoeuvre and bluff to avoid the inevitable coup. Abruptly changing roles and identities, he now took his Cuban machine-gun in hand to go down fighting in the presidential palace. It ensured that Chile, unlike Indonesia, went down in contemporary history with the forces of legitimate government holding off the forces of dictatorship to the very end.

Terror had an impact on the entire population. The basic premise of

The National Security Doctrine

'Many people find it difficult to admit that the world is living in a permanent state of war', wrote Colonel (now General) Bacigalupo of the National Security Academy in the inaugural number of its journal *National Security*. The ideology of National Security is a response to this lack of awareness on the part of the Latin American people. Its purpose is to show them that the state of war defines their human condition, and prepares them for the consequences.

When he drew up the outline of his government's programme in a speech on 11 September 1976, General Pinochet based his whole argument on this fact. In November 1976, an officer in the government's communications service sent out a circular to all national institutions to remind the country that, 'Today the world is at war. Soviet imperialism is extending its sphere of domination bit by bit, through a war of conquest which uses all known forms of moral, spiritual and physical aggression'.

At the meeting of the commanders-in-chief of the Latin American armed forces held in Montevideo in 1975, the head of the Brazilian armed forces, General Fritz de Asevedo Manso, reaffirmed that the world was at war and that this was a total war. But he was only repeating what his predecessor had said at the previous conference in September 1973.

So what is this war which military regimes invoke as the reason for their existence and ultimate test of their politics? The key word is 'total': it is a 'total war' we are involved in. This is the kind of war which communism has imposed upon us whether we like it or not. As the officer in charge of this government's communications network says, 'Nobody wants to live in a state of emergency, but the MIR and the communists have declared open war on us with no reason and no end'.

Three basic concepts seem to lie behind the doctrine of National Security. All of them are of US origin, or at least they come to us through the US. Their ultimate origins lie in France and Germany. *Generalized war, cold war,* and *revolutionary war* are the three concepts.

Generalized war is defined by the commanders-in-chief of the US forces as 'armed conflict between the great powers in which all the resources of the belligerents are used, and the national survival of one of them is in danger'.

Today, however, war takes the form of *cold war*. Its forms are new, but all the characteristics of war apply to it, and the armed forces must respond to it with an adequate strategy. This cold war is a permanent war. It operates at all levels, military, political, economic and psychological, only avoiding direct military

▶

confrontation. The doctrine of National Security is a response to precisely this kind of war. In Latin America, the concept of the cold war is law. According to the doctrine of National Security, our countries are at war with 'international communism'.

It is in the United States too that the idea of *revolutionary war* was conceived. It has subsequently become the favourite theme of Latin American officers since the training colleges for officers and soldiers were set up in the Panama Canal zone. This concept began its triumphant march across the Americas in 1961-1962. The revolutionary war is the new strategy of international communism. Wherever there is a revolutionary war, there one will find communism. Thus we reach the third principle, namely that revolutionary war is simply a new technique for waging war.

So one has to understand the technique well enough to be able to evolve efficient counter-techniques, and roll the revolutionary war back against its authors. US strategy operated as if the Vietnamese were objects in the hands of Russian technicians waging a revolutionary war. The only problem was to be more ingenious than the Russians. For such a strategy, the wars and outbreaks of violence in the Third World can be understood quite well without any reference to the history of their peoples.

Fr. Jose Comblin, 'The Doctrine of National Security' in *Two Essays on National Security*, Vicaría de Solidaridad, 1979.

a totalitarian society is apathy based on fear, and Chile was introduced to this new reality in 1973. Its population internalized the new law: *don't interfere whatever they do to your neighbours.* Urban slum-dwellers, peasants and workers were the worst affected. The first Christian Democrat victim of the repression was a trade unionist in the docks, killed within days of the coup for refusing to obey a military order and organizing a strike. In the rural areas, the local police were often induced to cooperate in a massacre by first getting them drunk. Many people unconnected with Popular Unity were among their victims. Much the same random factor was introduced in urban areas, when the police or neighbours were moved by the prevailing climate of hysteria to denounce those who looked suspicious as foreign agents or guerrillas — they often got it wrong. Workers who had been politically active were dismissed in droves after the coup, and the Chilean right set about computerizing its own list of 'pariahs'.

From just over three per cent at the time of the coup, economic unemployment in Santiago soared to over ten per cent in June 1974, before any government policies had taken effect. Meanwhile, wages

45

were dictated by government decree, and the activities of trade union officials (those few who survived the initial wave of arrests and dismissals), were severely circumscribed by law as well as by fear. In years to come, Chile's 'trade union leaders', the public figures who survived the repression and who had led the *gremio* opposition to Allende, were to operate in a vacuum, with no chance for their members to voice any complaints.

While the economic opportunities open to most people were collapsing, Chile's officer corps found itself with an enormous number of new career opportunities as managers of state-owned factories and firms, mayors of municipalities, deans of universities, and senior administrators in the civilian departments of state. Formerly a country with a proud professional tradition in every field, Chile was rapidly being militarized. From the armed forces' point of view, the risk in this process was the danger of losing its professionalism. This was seen as particularly serious since Chile faced hostile enemies on both its land borders. The fear that Peru and Argentina might combine against it in a bid to seize some part of Chile's national territory set limits on the 'politicization' of Chile's armed forces as a body, just as it helped reinforce General Pinochet's power as commander-in-chief.

Nevertheless, as different civilian groups assiduously began to court any officer they could find for his support in internal struggles over policy, some degree of politicization was inevitable. In 1976, the army was to take steps to professionalize its own political role, and to train future managers of the state, with the erection of a National Security Academy modelled on Brazil's famous war academy, the *Escola do Guerra*.

The Pinochet and the Chicago Coups within the Coup

The repression was essentially aimed at cutting out the Marxist cancer and restoring Chile to sanity, as General Leigh put it. The new military regime still needed a decision-making structure and a coherent set of policies.

Until the application of the Chicago shock treatment in 1975, Chile was governed in theory and in reality by a four-man junta composed of the heads of the different branches of the armed forces: General Pinochet, head of the army; General Leigh, head of the air force; Admiral Merino, head of the navy; and the man who until the coup was seventh in command in the police *(Carabineros)*, General Mendoza. A kind of gentlemen's understanding existed that the head of the junta was merely *primus inter pares*, and even that the position might rotate. This reflected the fact that no discussions on a structure of government had been held between the four branches before the navy and the air force precipitated the coup. Nevertheless, Pinochet naturally assumed the role of head of the junta as head of the armed forces, a title which he inherited equally naturally as commander-in-chief of the army. In any government based on internal military power, the army was bound to be the dominant political force, but over the next year Pinochet's own appetite for power enabled it to consolidate its hold over defence and the apparatus of repression. The way was prepared for a Pinochet coup within the coup.

The government functioned without a legislature, through decrees given the force of law. Nevertheless, a rough and ready division of labour was established from the beginning. The navy, possessors of the plan, took economic affairs. The air force took social issues, and the *carabineros* took over labour and agriculture, reflecting perhaps an early decision that these areas would require extensive policing. The members of the junta quickly established legislative committees to cover their respective areas, with civilian contacts and advisers playing a crucial role in determining who was appointed and what policy was followed. From the very beginning, however, Pinochet was extra-ordinarily secretive about his own civilian advisers, calling them in privately without consulting the rest of the junta. Later, this was to be the private road which people from Chile's old fascist network such as Pablo Rodriguez were to take in their quest for influence and power.

Nevertheless, as civilian advisers from all Chile's right-wing parties flocked into the government, jockeying for power, the rather uncouth, badly briefed Pinochet seemed overshadowed by Leigh and Merino, and it was they who were courted. Jaime Guzman, for example, established himself as Leigh's political adviser and gave a distinctly corporatist tone to the latter's early statements. It was also Leigh who brought in such sympathizers of the original Spanish *Falange* as Gaston Acuna and 'Alexis' Puga to head the government's communications agency, DINACOS. They retained these positions of power until the Letelier scandal. It was also Leigh who set up a commission to draft a new constitution which, according to him, was to give direct legislative participation to the *gremios* of women, youth and the armed forces. At this early stage it was Pinochet who talked of returning Chile to its traditional democracy.

Institutional factors and more simple personality differences were to change this situation. The air force and the navy were both more democratic institutions than the army. The head of the air force, in particular, encouraged frank and open discussion among his generals not a good basis for selling a fascist model of power. It was the army, with its traditions of absolute obedience, which most nearly matched the fascist demand for no dispersal of power and a glorification of the head of state. Coincidentally, that same centralization of power in the hands of a dictatorial force was to become necessary to the Chicago Boys, who were to find the air force's advocacy of social issues and the division of labour which gave them a certain independence in this field impossible to square with their own calls for an economic revolution.

Pinochet's own personality underlined this institutional reality, making the choices absolutely clear. He was an autocrat, not a man for discussion or compromise. He was prone to banging the table with his gun and shouting at other members of the junta when crossed. Merino and Mendoza were quickly overawed. Only General Leigh made any consistent attempt to oppose the centralization of power in Pinochet's hands, and although Leigh tried throughout 1974 to forge an alliance with Merino on many issues, the latter's weakness robbed the alliance of any force.

Slowly in the months after the coup, key advisers both from the extreme corporatist or *duro* side of the spectrum and from the *blandos* pushing the Chicago model began to gravitate towards Pinochet, convinced that he alone had the power to put their proposals into practice. Meanwhile, Pinochet was efficiently consolidating his own power base, placing army personnel on whose loyalty he could rely into key administrative positions.

The first dramatic step towards the new authoritarian model was taken in June 1974. Pinochet succeeded in consolidating the internal security forces of the army, navy and air force, into a single force, the DINA, which was in effect Chile's secret police. Controlled by the army and staffed in part by sympathizers of Fatherland and Freedom, the DINA grew enormously in personnel, finance and power. It began to acquire its own apparatus of professional advisers, psychologists, sociologists, economists, and political scientists, as well as experts in the more humdrum business of surveillance, torture and murder. Most importantly, this new empire was responsible only to Pinochet. Its head was Manuel Contreras, an aide and close personal friend through Pinochet's wife. Contreras reported personally to him daily, and also had the use of a direct closed-circuit television link.

In June 1974 Pinochet formally took on the role of president of the junta. By December, he had manoeuvred himself into position as president of Chile. Efforts by Leigh to prevent this takeover failed.

The process by which the Chicago Boys manoeuvred themselves into an equally clear dominance on the economic front was rather more complex. They were the authors of the 'navy' plan on the economy, but that plan had barely been read by the new military government when it took power, in spite of the fact that each junta member had a copy the morning after the coup. The first cabinet was entirely composed of military men, who had little or no experience of government and very little understanding of public affairs. Chile's constitutional position itself had ensured that the armed forces had no education in issues of economic development. Those generals most sympathetic to strategies of national economic development had either been murdered (like Schneider), or were disqualified (like General Prats), due to their involvement with the Allende regime. Naturally therefore, civilian advisers played the dominant role in determining policy. How advisers were acquired by the new power brokers, and how the occupants of key positions secured them, was very much a hit-and-miss process depending as much on personal contacts as on the sort of advice they could be expected to provide.

There was a rush to take up the coveted position of adviser, whether for ideological reasons or for personal gain. Businessmen rushed to CORFO to offer their services, sensing that the process of privatization would be crucial to their own financial and industrial interests. Members of the landowners' organization, the SNA, did the same at the ministry of agriculture.

Some made mistakes they were to regret. Orlando Saenz, president of SOFOFA and Monday Club member, made a major error of political judgement. He had decided that the navy was the crucial force and had become adviser to Admiral Huerta at the ministry of foreign affairs. This meant he spent his time abroad instead of carving out a local power base. Within eight months he was to attempt to return to power and reverse the tide flowing in Chicago's direction. He used Pablo Rodriguez's personal contacts to gain the ear of Pinochet himself and suggest a more interventionist and nationalist approach. Pinochet at this point seemed disposed to agree with him, but while the general was to flirt periodically with extreme nationalist political models throughout the ensuing decade, he was never to be so energetically committed even to mild nationalist models in economics. The Chicago school was in the ascendant.

There were good reasons for this. Of all the groups, the Chicago Boys were the best placed, the most cohesive, the best disciplined, and had the clearest idea of what should be done. They also revived a familiar policy of keeping a think-tank in reserve as a focus for spreading ideas and training ambitious young recruits.

Thus, shortly after the coup, Chicago Boys were spread throughout the crucial economic departments and in some non-economic departments as well. Sergio de Castro entered the ministry of the economy as an adviser. Andres Sanfuentes and Jose Luis Zabala went back to the central bank. At the ministry of finance, Juan Villarzu obtained the key post of director of the budget; Roberto Kelly, the original go-between for the Monday Club and the navy over the first plan, became head of the national planning office (ODEPLAN) and turned it into the Chicago think-tank and the new training centre for its technical experts, from which they would sally forth to take control of the rest of the state machine.

Each economic decision was a political battle which had to be passed to the junta for final arbitration. The Chicago Boys became experts at explaining to bemused military men why the *peso* (which was introduced as the unit of currency in September 1975, replacing the *escudo*) had to be devalued and why prices had to be freed from artificial controls. Eventually the junta decided that they needed a civilian to take charge of the economy.

Here, luck intervened. Leigh recommended a personal contact of his and one of the founding fathers of the national development agency (CORFO), Raul Saez, as minister of the economy. Saez was unable to take up the post immediately, and he in turn recommended Fernando Leniz, director of *El Mercurio* and one of Chile's leading businessmen, for the post. Leniz thus became the first civilian minister of the economy under the new military government, and with Sergio de Castro as his adviser in effect bought the Chicago plan. The coup had been carried out, and with *El Mercurio's* support, even assured.

Economic policies began to bear more clearly the Chicago imprint. Prices continued to be freed while wages remained frozen. The peso was further devalued. Steps toward the establishment of a private capital market were taken when interest rates in the state-owned banking sector were frozen and private finance companies allowed to offer a rate more than 15 per cent higher. This led to a flood of personal savings from the state sector into private hands, thus providing the foundation of new fortunes for Javier Vial and Manuel Cruzat. Taxes on profits were eliminated, and indirect taxes introduced to finance state expenditure. A new private investment code was set up with the aim of attracting private foreign capital, and compensation was agreed with the US copper companies for the nationalized copper mines.

In January 1974 a key policy was announced, 'to end indiscriminate protection . . . and to modify substantially the tariff policy in order to improve efficiency in the Chilean productive system and to make it competitive internationally within three years'. At that time few businessmen apart from Vial and Cruzat believed that such a programme could be accomplished. Meanwhile, the IMF, the World Bank, US banks and multinationals were sending their teams to offer advice and give their seal of approval to the general direction being taken.

Within the ranks of the Chicago Boys, however, tensions were

WARNING:
Politics is bad for your health.
Ministry of the Interior.

Source: Hoy 6 January 1982

emerging, reflecting the fact that Christian Democracy was gradually being pushed into opposition. The party had supported the coup. Its press and radio had remained silent throughout the first months of repression and torture. However, privately and through internal documents, most of which fell into the hands of the junta, Christian Democrat leaders were expressing concern. President Frei's offer of his services to the head of the new junta on the day of the coup had been snubbed, and the junta resented the Christian Democrats' apparent belief that the armed forces had carried out the coup to hand it over in a neat package to the ex-president. There was to be no royal road for the Christian Democrats into positions of power. In fact, repression had already begun to claim Christian Democrat victims.

Policy differences were also emerging. Essentially, the Christian Democrats were determined to preserve both some level of social expenditure and their favourite experimental forms of economic property ownership, such as cooperatives and share participation schemes. They were hoping to avoid the extreme concentration of private property which a full-blooded Chicago model was bound to produce.

As the Christian Democrats were moving into opposition, the power of Christian Democrat advisers in the government became weaker, even though these had initially exercised apparent control over three powerful bodies, the ministry of finance, the ministry of labour and the central bank. Party members hoped that the appointment of Jorge Cauas, a Christian Democrat, as minister of finance in 1974 might strengthen their position. But Cauas immediately resigned from the party, and the Christian Democrat advisers in his ministry and the central bank left soon afterwards. In Cauas's publicly expressed view, which was the same as that of Sergio de Castro and the other Chicago Boys, the pace of change suggested by the Christian Democrat party, particularly in terms of privatization and reduction of state expenditures, was much too slow.

The freeing of prices and devaluation of the peso had meanwhile given a dramatic boost to inflation. In the last quarter of 1973, prices rose by a fantastic 128 per cent. In 1974, the quarterly index of prices fell back to a 45 per cent average, still an enormous figure. Inflation is of course one of the *bêtes noires* of the Chicago school. Nevertheless, 'repressed inflation', price rises held down by state controls, is if anything worse in Chicago eyes than inflation itself. These were therefore policies designed to allow market forces to re-establish the 'correct' or 'natural' price structure for the economy, one which would be in line with the international structure of relative prices, a crucial step towards the open economy favoured by Chicago economists. The increase in prices when wages were frozen also helped to restore profitability and redistributed income from the poor to the rich. Allowing inflation to rise in this way also had another purpose. The freeing of prices was so inflationary that it led to a climate of opinion which favoured drastic cuts in state expenditure and tariffs, themselves the two critical elements in the Chicago Plan.

However, cutting state expenditure proved difficult. In practice, military men who depend on the state for their livelihood are naturally more inclined to favour state expenditure. Furthermore, when it came to the departments for which they were now responsible, they resented having their responsibilities cut or privatized. In the first six months of 1974 the price of copper was at record levels and there seemed no real need to cut back state spending, which would only have added to rising unemployment and created a spate of unnecessary bankruptcies. The Chicago model looked as though it might become bogged down in the sheer morass of opposition it faced, detail by detail and objection by objection.

Then, in the middle of 1974, economic misfortune came to their aid. The price of copper fell from 126 cents per pound to 78 cents per pound. By the end of 1974 it was 62 cents per pound. This fall, together with the increase in the price of oil, put immediate pressure on Chile's balance of payments. At the end of 1974, net balance of payments reserves were US$375 million in the red.

Inflation began to accelerate again, slowly in 1974 and then more quickly by March 1975, as the government tried to keep up its expenditure in the face of falling revenues and dramatically increased the money supply. Using all their influence in the media, the Chicago Boys pointed out that drastic solutions were necessary to halt the inflationary spiral and solve the balance of payments crisis. They called this solution the 'programme for economic recovery'. It was the political opportunity for 'shock'.

6 The Shock 1975-1976

Shock Treatment

Preparations for 'shock treatment' had begun long before the official text of the government Economic Recovery Programme was released on 24 April 1975. This treatment involved the deliberate creation of a massive deflation through a drastic cut in public expenditure which would cause mass unemployment, wage cuts, bankruptcies and widespread deprivation. The Chicago Boys had been debating the merits of the treatment for almost a year prior to the April announcement. As early as June 1974, *El Mercurio* had outlined the two basic solutions for inflation as gradualism versus 'shock' (just as Hayek was to outline them to Mrs Thatcher in December 1980). (See Box Page 55). By November 1974, the newspaper had come out in support of the latter.

Shock treatment was much more than a response to a balance of payments crisis caused by a rise in oil prices and a fall in the price of Chile's basic export. Normally, this kind of crisis would have led to an appeal to the IMF for a loan, and an IMF-style package of deflation. 'Shock' went further than even the hard-nosed, cynical men of the IMF regarded as feasible. It was meant not only to strengthen Chile's hand in world markets by stimulating new, non-traditional exports of the goods no longer being consumed within Chile. More important still, it was designed to force acceptance of the Chicago economic model. State expenditure was to be reshaped in a fashion which would ensure that Chile would no longer depend on what Hayek calls artificial stimulation by the government to keep its economy going. Structures and expectations were both to be revolutionized. As Javier

Vial, the president of the BHC empire (See Box Page 72) said in
February 1975: 'The worst problem is the mentality of Chileans, who
are not ready for firms to have complete freedom. It's a problem of
mediocrity, the bureaucratic mentality, the belief that the state will
look after it . . .' 'Shock' was to change all that.

Prior to the announcement of 'shock', a high-powered seminar was
organized by BHC. It was a meeting of what had become a new
'*laissez-faire* international' (See Box Page 56). Milton Friedman,
Arnold Harberger, and Carlos Langoni (leading Brazilian economist

The international web of the new laissez-faire

There is a spider's web of connections between the theorists and practitioners of the new *laissez-faire*, a web which stretches across many countries and covers different continents.

The spider at the centre of the web has undoubtedly been Friedrich Von Hayek. Hayek has been the most consistent critic of Keynes and Keynesianism from as far back as 1931 to an article in the *Economist* in 1983 where he claims that Keynes was 'wholly wrong'. Behind theoretical disagreements lies Hayek's belief that Keynesian policies are an inevitable step down the road to totalitarianism, whether fascist or socialist.

In 1944, Hayek published *The Road to Serfdom*, attacking the policies which would provide the basis for Labour's 1945 manifesto. The phrase was taken up by Churchill during his election campaign, and Margaret Thatcher, who claims to have been profoundly influenced by *The Road to Serfdom*, reiterated the theme in her 1983 election campaign.

In 1947, Hayek met with 38 like-minded intellectuals at Mont Pelerin in Switzerland to discuss 'the crisis of our times', created by 'the growth of a view of history which denies all absolute moral standards and by the growth of theories which question the desirability of the rule of law . . . by a decline of belief in private property and the competitive market.'

Milton Friedman was among those founding members of the Mont Pelerin Society, and one of its future presidents, after Hayek stepped down from the presidency in 1960. Meetings have been held all over Europe and in the United States, Japan, Guatemala, Venezuela, and in 1981 in Chile. It is now a society with over 600 members across the world.

The Mont Pelerin Society spawned a number of institutes and centres designed to influence policy and policy-makers: in Argentina, the Centre for Studies in Liberty, and in Britain, the Institute for Economic Affairs, founded in 1955, which in turn stimulated Margaret Thatcher and Sir Keith Joseph to found the Centre for Policy Studies in 1975. Members of the centre visited Chile to learn from its experiences, and some of their publications have been reprinted in sympathetic Chilean journals. In 1980, making their second attempt at such an organization, Chile's new ideologues of *laissez-faire* established their own Centre for Policy Studies (*Centro de Estudios Públicos*) with Friedrich Von Hayek as its honorary president.

Chile's initial link with this web goes back to 1955, when a US aid

➧

agency financed a link between the economics department of the Catholic University of Santiago and the economics department of the University of Chicago. This was done to combat the influence of the Economic Commission for Latin America's (ECLA) structuralist ideas, the Latin American version of Keynes, which blamed inflation on structural weaknesses in the underlying economy and called for state intervention to foster industrialization and undertake fundamental structural reforms. ECLA had also rejected the doctrine of comparative advantage, which justified the United States' pre-eminence in international trade and finance. Under the influence of both Friedrich Von Hayek and Milton Friedman, the University of Chicago had become the mecca for the new *laissez-faire*, combining education in sophisticated mathematical techniques and technical economics with the overall ideology of the new 'libertarianism'.

Chicago taught these young economists that inflation is a purely monetary phenomenon caused solely by demand factors. It also taught them that economic liberty is more fundamental than political liberty — ideas as closely associated with Hayek and his philosophical works such as *The Constitution of Liberty* (1960) as 'monetarism' is associated with Friedman. The tendency of the Chicago Boys to demonstrate Chile's glorious economic prospects by projecting a mathematical curve rising high and far into the future has more to do with Friedman's mathematical enthusiasm than anything Hayek would countenance. The idea that Pinochet's 1981 constitution be called the *'Constitución de la Libertad'* was borrowed directly from Hayek's ambitious work on the state with the same title. It is revealing that Hayek never disassociated himself from this plagiarism.

It was from this link that Chile developed a powerful group of economists known locally as the 'Chicago Boys'. Returning to Chile, the new economic prophets created the Centre for Social and Economic Studies in 1964, to influence elite opinion as a think-tank for the right in the 1970 presidential elections. Though they established useful and enduring links with the business community during this period, many businessmen still found their ideas too extreme, and impossible to implement within a democracy.

The links help to explain why, after 1973, Chile became the purest example of the new *laissez-faire* model. The international web of contacts lent its full support to the Chilean experiment. Key figures like Milton Friedman, Hayek himself, and Arnold Harberger, a Chicago economist married to a Chilean who was the spiritual godfather of many of the Chicago Boys, appeared in Chile, often to throw their weight behind their proteges at crucial political moments.

and ideologue of the Brazilian model, now president of its central bank) among others, arrived in Santiago to lend their prestige to the shock policy.

Friedman played down any notion that Chile's economic difficulties might be due to temporary dislocations in the international economy, caused for instance by the shock to world economic equilibrium of OPEC's second massive increase in the price of oil. 'No', he said, 'the problems of Chile are manufactured in this country'. According to Friedman, 'the policy of applying poultices instead of amputating the diseased limb brings with it the danger of a much more painful final outcome than the pains one was trying to avoid along the way . . .'; 'Chile has two choices: a very high temporary level of unemployment, or a very long period of high unemployment'. The diseased limb, of course, was the state sector.

Another important theme of the conference was that 'shock' would lead to an economic miracle. As Langoni explained it, cutting state expenditure had been the key to the Brazilian success story (a view which represents a highly tendentious presentation of the role of the state in Brazil). It was Langoni too, who emphasized the need for an iron will to carry the government through the inevitable period of public misunderstanding.

Throughout his stay in Chile, during which he saw Pinochet and some ministers, Friedman constantly reiterated the basic message. Chile must cut state expenditure by 20 per cent. Gradualism was no alternative. He stated: 'The immediate cause of inflation is always a larger increase in the amount of money than in production . . ., and this is clearly the Chilean case. The first necessity therefore is to end inflation, and the only way Chile can do this is by cutting the fiscal deficit, preferably by reducing public expenditure . . . In Chile, gradualism seems to me impossible'.

Pinochet bought the package. A distinguished international economist had personally assured him that an economic boom would follow if the medicine were applied. Appeals to iron will, to toughness, to not giving in to social pressures, all fitted in remarkably well with his personal self-image. More important still, the alternative (particularly as presented by Orlando Saenz) implied a more gradualist, interventionist policy with the assistance of foreign loans, and was a problem. Chile had become isolated in the world community, condemned by the International Labour Organization (ILO) for its repression of trade unions and by the United Nations for its violation of human rights. Foreign loans might imply humiliating conditions. They might even entail accepting a timetable for a return to democracy. Not surprisingly, Pinochet saw his own position as best secured by the Chicago formula, which promised him freedom from outside interference in his government, and sufficient reserves to fund adequate purchases of arms.

Chicago and Pinochet: the Emergence of a Personal Dictatorship

'Shock' provided the occasion for reinforcing both Pinochet's personal authority as president, and the political position of the Chicago Boys as his preferred advisers. An economic dictatorship was created which drew entirely on the Chicago theorists within the government for its personnel. Leniz, who later claimed that he fully supported the shock programme, but who was nevertheless associated with a more gradualist package and a more populist personal style, was removed from his post as minister of the economy. Jorge Cauas was appointed a kind of super-minister with total control over most of the spending departments. The progress of the new programme was monitored on a daily basis by Cauas and three other Chicago Boys: Sergio de Castro, now minister of the economy, Pablo Baraona, the new president of the central bank, and Roberto Kelly, head of ODEPLAN. Alvaro Bardon, author of the *El Mercurio* article in favour of 'shock', entered the central bank as vice-president.

'Shock' marked the end of any Christian Democrat participation in the government. Juan Villarzu left as director of the budget, and was replaced by Juan Carlos Mendez, an enthusiastic supporter of Hayek's political philosophy and a much more reliable Chicago Boy. Alvaro Bardon, like Cauas before him, formally resigned from the Christian Democrats.

It was indicative of the new style of government inaugurated when Pinochet became president of Chile that the shock policies were pushed through with virtually no discussion. Before the cabinet meeting which discussed the package, potential opponents such as Raul Saez were carefully kept in ignorance of what was being proposed until the meeting itself, and the policies were rushed through so quickly that objections could hardly be voiced.

Nor were any questions raised in the armed forces. Pinochet informed his generals, none of whom complained. The key group of army generals behind the coup had by now nearly all resigned or been retired. General Bonilla, for example, died mysteriously in a helicopter crash in March 1975. Generals Palacio, Nuño, and Toro, all of whom represented a different economic philosophy, had already left the armed forces. General Arellano Stark, increasingly isolated, offered his resignation in October 1975 and was allowed to resign the following January. No serious potential rivals from the pre-coup period remained on active service. Junior officers were locked into a tradition which stressed obedience and loyalty rather than discussion, and were furthermore handicapped in making any objections by the ethos that 'the armed forces must be kept out of politics' to look after its professional duties. This formula gave total political power to Pinochet.

Thus the only military men to discuss the shock programme openly among themselves were the air force generals. Here, the atmosphere of a deliberately created and sustained national emergency came to Pinochet's aid. In the face of some dissent, Leigh decided in April 1975 to back the programme, on the grounds that the necessary social costs would have to be paid to defeat inflation. By the end of August, he had decided that this was wrong, and publicly proclaimed the cost of the new economic model to be too high. But on this and other occasions, his decision came too late to halt the tide of events.

The need to conciliate Leigh, the one active source of potential opposition within the junta, may explain why the ministry of labour did not come under the Chicago mandate. The air force had taken over the ministry in mid-1975, when the prospect of an ILO mission in less than five months time made it convenient to end the nightmare of confusion and repression of the previous nine months. Bitterly opposed to the Christian Democrats as politicians and political manipulators, the air force was nonetheless an enthusiastic supporter of their ideas on labour relations. Thus in January 1975, before 'shock' was introduced, General Leigh himself presented a bill on 'Workers' Participation in the Firm' to the media. In May, labour minister Nicanor Diaz presented a draft Labour Code to the unions for their comments. Although the draft profoundly upset the unions by its proposals for a drastic reshaping of the existing labour movement (which they would certainly have found traumatic) it did assume a return to union elections and collective bargaining in the near future. Furthermore, it did not assume either that strikes should be abolished, which was one of Pinochet's most favoured objectives, or that unions should be stripped of all economic power, which was the Chicago Boys' (and Hayek's) view. Pinochet had in fact listened sympathetically to the fascists' ideas both for a trade union school to instruct new generations of union leaders in the doctrine of National Security, and for a *Secretario de los Gremios*, to mobilize trade union support for the government as well as help the secret police to control any trade union opposition before it could acquire real strength. However, in the face of Diaz's opposition and the presence of the ILO, these projects continued only in an unofficial fashion or were postponed.

Since June 1974, when Leigh himself had come out in favour of a

60

political system which incorporated the old political parties, the air force had also emerged as the principal military advocate of an early return to democracy. As guardians of this new order *in utero*, they were opposed to any existing political force using labour to carve itself out a power base. Above all, they were opposed to any attempt to consolidate the military regime as a permanent feature of political life. General Diaz in particular mounted a personal crusade against the small fascist sects in the ministry of labour, for this very reason. Pinochet, whose ambition was to die like Franco, still in power, was much more sympathetically inclined towards Francoists who talked to him about the importance of building an official labour movement in the Spanish mould.

Here again, 'shock' reinforced Pinochet's personal control. In mid-June 1975, the ministry of the interior publicly took over the task of controlling trade union activities with a series of well-publicized arrests of trade unionists. Among those arrested were 11 Christian Democrat union activists at the El Salvador copper mine. Diaz's ability to preserve trade unions from the worst ravages of the DINA was henceforth almost non-existent. 1976 was to be the worst year for trade union repression throughout the decade, with the exception of the few months surrounding the 1973 coup. In July, Pinochet also postponed introduction of the new Labour Code. In October, speaking at a meeting of workers at El Teniente at the request of his most loyal trade union supporter, Guillermo Medina, he made his position crystal-clear. There could be no union elections because, like all elections, they would create disharmony, and because 'next they will be asking me for elections to congress'. In March 1976 Diaz was removed from the labour ministry and replaced by a civilian, Sergio Fernandez, who had no other institutional support than the personal favour of the president himself.

But if, as you say, you represent the silent majority, why all this tremendous outlay on tanks, submachine guns, bombs, grenades etc?

That's to keep our support intact . . . by keeping the majority silent.

Source: Análisis Aug/Sept 1979

Throughout the period of 'shock', Pinochet's authority over Chile's political processes grew ever more absolute, and through him, so too did that of the 'Chicago revolution' which had his personal approval. Leigh and the air force had been marginalized. The DINA was a personal fief of the president. The only vocal opposition to his policies allowed, the voices of Orlando Saenz and Pablo Rodriguez writing in *La Tercera*, were tolerated because they appealed directly to Pinochet on a personal basis, speaking to him as though he had nothing to do with an economic project which rested entirely on his personal assent. *El Mercurio* countered by suggesting that non-economists should be barred from commenting publicly on economic affairs, on the grounds that non-medics would not be allowed to comment on medical matters. The Christian Democrats were muzzled and in disarray, nervous of becoming victims of the repression of a coup which they had done so much to create. In March 1976 their internal theoretical journal *Politica y Espiritu* was closed down, never to reappear. *Ercilla* was also bought up in 1976 by Javier Vial's BHC business empire, and converted into another voice for orthodox economics and support for Pinochet.

At this moment, when the danger of Chile becoming a new personal dictatorship was at its greatest, the Catholic Church stepped in. As the repression began to reach deep into the ranks of loyal Catholics and Christian Democrats as well as Marxists, and the level of suffering among the poor and ordinary workers which was daily confronting its own priests grew intolerable, it took decisive action. In November 1975 the cardinal effectively dissolved the existing umbrella organization, the *Comité Pro Paz*, which had been set up a month after the coup and united all Chile's churches in the defence of human rights victims. In its place, he set up an organization which had a broader and more specifically Catholic social and political mandate, the *Vicaría de Solidaridad*. This began to undertake the essential tasks of building a loose network of emergency social services in those areas where it was possible — children's canteens, for instance, to temper the worst effects of starvation in the shanty-towns. It also began to rally the forces of opposition, particularly among the trade unions, fostering and publicizing both right-wing Christian Democrat trade union leaders who gathered together in the 'Group of Ten', and left-wing Christian Democrat and Marxist trade union leaders who formed the *Coordinadora Nacional Sindical* (CNS).

Simultaneously, the church began an ideological offensive on the twin pillars of the new society: the *laissez-faire* model of economics, and the National Security doctrine. In a series of publications and public declarations, it attacked both: the first, for turning economic science into a new form of ideology, and the latter for sacrificing the interests and basic security of individuals to the supposed greater causes of the state.

The Economic and Social Consequences

Government expenditure was cut by 27 per cent in 1975, and capital investment fell by 50 per cent. Tax receipts were increased by the removal of exemptions from VAT and public sector prices were raised. Inflation was hardly 'stopped dead': the consumer price index fell from 369.2 in 1974 to 343.3 in 1975. However, the upward trend in prices was clearly reversed, and in 1976 the consumer price index fell to 198, and continued to fall thereafter. As internal demand collapsed, so did imports, and the growth of 'non-traditional' exports began to compensate for the fall in the price of copper exports. Pinochet achieved the desired balance of payments surplus and the protection from outside political intervention in the first quarter of 1976.

The cost was an incredible fall of 16.6 per cent in Chile's GNP, perhaps a world record outside times of war. Industrial production was worst hit, as some Chilean industries disappeared, never to appear again. Wages continued to fall as they had done since the coup. In the industrial sector, wages fell from an index of 100 in 1970 to 47.9 in 1975. Not surprisingly, with lower wage costs and massive redundancies, productivity in those firms which survived shot up.

The social effects of 'shock' were catastrophic. By the beginning of 1976, unemployment officially stood at 19.8 per cent. If one adds to these figures the numbers working on a government emergency public works programme known as the Minimum Employment Programme (PEM) the total rose to 28 per cent. Chile's already ramshackle social security service broke down almost completely, as firms going into bankruptcy defaulted automatically on their social security insurance payments, and the government in turn refused to pay unemployment benefits to those made redundant. Old contracts of employment which guaranteed a fixed sum for years of service were dishonoured without compunction. Particularly in the urban shanty-towns, unemployment reached levels unheard of in Chilean history, in some cases of 80 per cent or more. (See Box Page 64). Only the church, through its soup kitchens, helped sustain these new poor. In the rich districts of Santiago, street corner after street corner was lined with girls selling their bodies to get food for themselves and their families.

Those firms which did survive were protected by a government policy of deliberately driving down wages. An automatic wage rise in line with inflation which was planned for mid-1975 was deliberately missed. Minimum wages had already been diminished substantially

The Cost of Monetarism

'The cost has been very unequally distributed. Workers have carried a much greater cost in unemployment and in lower wages than the fall in product *per capita* would warrant, even those among the 20 per cent poorest of the population. What this means is that other groups have not only not had to make any sacrifices, but must actually have made gains in real income . . .

This inequality in the distribution of social costs cannot be explained away by saying that the price of copper today is half what it was a year ago, because although that might explain why the total cost was so high, it wouldn't explain why workers were paying the bulk of it. While production fell 12 per cent *per capita* between 1970 and 1975, private consumption actually fell less, by 11 per cent *per capita*. Meanwhile, the real income of workers fell between 30 and 40 per cent.

The disproportionate fall in the cost of labour has allowed industrialists to make a greater profit margin on each unit sold, which has tended to compensate them for the fall in production.'

Joseph Ramos, University of Chile, September 1975

'How many times have I heard this phrase which sends shivers down my back: "Father, I've thought that the best thing would be if I and the children were to die . . ." I think of the mother who spent five days giving her child nothing but bottles of clear tea, with or without sugar . . .'

Mensaje, November 1975

'It is normal for the children who use these children's canteens to eat only this one meal during the entire day . . . Many take the bread home with them. They give it to their mothers, and the mother gives it back to them for supper . . . It's a new custom which has sprung up in this struggle for subsistence . . .'

Mensaje, July 1976

'According to the official price of bread at 2.50 pesos per kilo and the official minimum wage of 0.41 pesos per hour, in December 1975, under the rules of the military junta and with the advice and

♦

> consent of their Chicago Boys and of you personally, Milton
> Friedman and Arnold Harberger, an hour's work buys 160 grams of
> bread and it is necessary to work more than six hours to buy one kilo
> of bread in Chile at the minimum wage — if you can get it!'
>
> Andre Gunder Frank, *Economic Genocide in Chile, Two Open
> Letters to Arnold Harberger and Milton Friedman,* 1976

by inflation and government wage policies following the coup. Now
they were driven down further still. In the public sector, where PEM
employees were largely taken on, the effect of the government's new
programme was to replace the existing legal minimum wage with
another lower one, in which wages far below what was necessary to
sustain a family were supplemented by food handouts. In the private
sector, subsidies were made available to firms which took on
additional workers, again at the minimum wage level.

The net effect of these policies was to produce the kind of
restructuring of expectations which the Chicago Boys considered a
fundamental part of their strategy. All job security and confidence in
future employment disappeared; workers would hereafter organize
their trade unions, when they were once again allowed to do so, in an
atmosphere of profound insecurity. The confidence of workers in
Chile's old security system was also destroyed, which was just as well,
since in ODEPLAN's analysis the extra 33 per cent it cost employers
on their wage bill was one of the crucial reasons why Chilean wages
were so much higher than the 'internationally prevailing levels' with
which they would have to compete from now on.

Employers, faced with the collapse of their internal markets, were
forced to adapt by finding markets abroad for their products. This
new strategy was hardly enough to save them from disastrous levels of
over-capacity, nor to prevent many firms from going bankrupt as the
level of debts necessary to keep them afloat soared. But it was enough
to give a decisive shift to Chile's export pattern, as fruits, vegetables
and wine and such basic consumer goods as shoes flowed abroad.
Structural reforms to emphasize this desired change in behaviour went
ahead throughout the 'shock' period. Tariffs were further reduced,
even though national industry could hardly survive in its own markets.
Privatization also continued, in a way that was bound to increase the
degree to which Chilean industry was concentrated in fewer and fewer
hands. As the banks were privatized, the rate of interest they were
allowed to charge was freed from state controls. The real rate of

interest soared to an incredible yearly equivalent of 178 per cent in the third quarter of 1975. Firms trying to borrow to stave off bankruptcy found themselves in even greater debt to the banks and finance companies. Amongst the most prominent of these were Javier Vial of BHC and Manuel Cruzat of Cruzat-Larrain, Chicago Boys with good personal contacts with those in charge of the privatization programme. Not surprisingly, these financiers managed to buy up much of Chilean industry at a remarkably cheap price, laying the basis for future business empires bigger than the country had known in its monopoly-dogged history. However, as *El Mercurio* said:

'Concentration of economic power is dangerous in a closed economy, but it hardly matters in an economy open to free international competition. What matters is efficiency. The important point is that groups who are suffering from the economic policy should not be able to obtain privileged or exceptional status, because that would affect the success of the economic experiment and make new concessions easier. The changes in mentality and income which the programme implies are so profound that only extraordinary national discipline can enable us to sustain them.'

Pinochet provided the discipline. Meanwhile, the concentration of economic power in the hands of Cruzat-Larrain and BHC went ahead.

The trauma which Chile's people were suffering increased during these nightmare years, as the poor faced hunger, and active opponents of the regime faced a new wave of 'disappearances'. *El Mercurio* however turned even these experiences to Chicago's advantage, arguing that they were yet another motive for carrying the programme forward:

'The principal cause of present problems is nothing more than the unchecked and irrational growth of the state apparatus, which the economy of this country should not subsidize by one further peso, if it wants to regain its health.'

7 Fool's Gold and Fool's Democracy

The Conjuror's Miracle

Pinochet himself formally announced the end of 'shock' on 29 June
1976:

'One year after the Economic Recovery Programme was undertaken, thanks
to the efforts of all Chileans, I can state today that we are truly independent
and that we have recovered our international credibility. There is a surplus in
our balance of payments and we have sufficient reserves and foreign credit to
meet any emergency.
   The country is entering a new phase, one of more intense activity, higher
employment, and a better standard of living for all Chileans.'

'Shock' had shifted the country in the desired direction. In Chile, the
three pillars of a Keynesian social order which were most anathema to
Hayek — a powerful state, a powerful working class, and a set of
strong barriers between the national economy and a world economy
whose unchannelled forces might upset government attempts to
exercise economic control, were crumbling.

   The state's economic and social activities had been drastically
curtailed. The private sector was now clearly the dominant force in
capital accumulation. This ended a 30-year era in which, following
models presented by ECLA, the state (through CORFO) had been
Chile's largest single investor, and had created many of its most
productive industries. By 1980 all but 15 of the 507 state firms in
Popular Unity's enlarged state sector had been privatized, though
copper, electricity, oil exploration and production and other giants
still remained to pose new headaches. Rather than the state funding
investment in these areas, however, the running of state businesses as

67

profit-maximizing concerns had ensured that they contributed to the state's fiscal surplus. Fiscal deficits were a thing of the past.

Through repression, and above all through the creation of a massive reserve army of unemployed people (which would never fall below ten per cent of Chile's active population, even at the peak of the boom) the political power of organized labour had been weakened. Clearly, if trade unions were legalized in the future, they would no longer be able to bid up the price of their members' wages through the exercise of monopoly powers. Nowhere was this better illustrated than in the manufacturing sector, where strikes could now be broken simply by increasing the imports of alternative supplies from abroad. The chief architect of the original plan and its *eminence grise*, Sergio de Castro, in his new role as minister of finance, pushed rapidly ahead with the reduction of tariffs.

Chile was to be an open economy, if necessary the most open economy in the world. By the end of 1978, Chile's average tariff stood at a mere ten per cent, lower than it had been even during the nineteenth century *laissez-faire* era. Pleas from industrialists to give them more time to adjust to the new order were ignored.

From December 1976 onwards, as the original team which had drafted the pre-coup plan took over the levers of power, with Baraona as minister of the economy and Bardon as president of the central bank, the economic miracle promised by Friedman and others appeared to be coming true. Growth rates certainly seemed miraculous: five per cent in 1976, 8.6 per cent in 1977, six per cent in 1978, and 8.5 per cent in 1979. It was the era of extravagant promises, when Jose Piñera, a future minister of labour, could make his reputation with the government by drawing a graph which extrapolated such rates of growth ever onwards and upwards. Pinochet promised that every Chilean would soon own a car, and Arnold Harberger flew in yet again to bask in the glory of his disciples, declaring solemnly, 'One can predict that in ten years Chileans will enjoy a standard of living similar to that of Spain, which has a domestic product at the moment about double Chile's, while in 20 years Chileans will possibly be enjoying the same standard of living as Holland . . .'

It was a fools' paradise, for there was a fatal flaw in the boom. It was not based on new productive investment. Chile's rate of fixed capital formation *per capita* remained at an all-time low, one of the lowest in Latin America. As inflation continued to fall, real wages and salaries began to rise again, fuelling the demand for goods and services. For a period this was easily met by drawing into production the massive spare capacity created by the 'shock' itself, particularly in industry. Increasingly, however, it was met by importing manufactured goods which local industry did not provide.

The key factor behind the boom which made such imports possible was an element never foreseen in the original Chicago plan drawn up before the coup, namely the contraction of massive foreign debts by the private sector. Those who drafted the original plan had hoped that Chile might emerge as a new Taiwan or South Korea, attracting private foreign investment in manufacturing by the cheapness of its skilled labour force. A private foreign investment code had been designed which was entirely favourable to the foreign investor; and by November 1976 Chile had withdrawn from the Andean Pact, finding its panoply of state controls over multinationals far too restrictive.

Chile though failed to attract very much attention from foreign investors. Any investment which did come into the country from foreign companies went almost entirely into minerals. The size of the local market was too small to offer any real incentive to the manufacturing multinationals, who could in any case export directly to Chile's unprotected markets. As for its cheap labour, they had the choice of a dozen better-situated countries with equally cheap wages throughout the world for their export platforms.

'I need a list of deportees.'

'I'm going chief.'

'Delinquents, detainees, disappeared . . . mmm . . . I'm afraid it's not here.'

'Have you looked under non-traditional exports?'

Source: Análisis July 1979

The Chilean economy was therefore increasingly forced back upon the products in which it had a natural comparative advantage, minerals and primary products such as wood, fruits and sea-food, harvested with cheap labour and requiring very little investment in processing. Nevertheless, the Chicago Boys had made an impression on the world banking community out of all proportion to Chile's real economic strengths. Here was an economic model after their own hearts, and the banks were in the best possible position to shower

69

'Workers are asking for a wage rise.'
'Well sack them.'
'But what about the social costs?'
'We're not paying them.'

Source: Hoy 8 July 1981

benefits upon a favoured son. Just as Chile emerged from the 'shock', world financial markets were suffering from an excess of liquidity. The massive increase in oil revenues obtained by the OPEC countries had been recycled through the Western banks, and with the Western economies themselves under the control of deflation-minded governments, the banks entered into a mad loaning spree to selected Third World countries.

In line with its total commitment to private enterprise and new faith in the private sector's entrepreneurial judgement, the Chilean government now removed all restrictions on the amount which Chilean banks and firms could borrow abroad. The dance of the millions had begun.

At its peak, money was flowing into Chile at the rate of US$3 million a day. Almost all of this consisted in loans from private international banks to private banks in Chile. Few loans if any went to the Chilean state for the large capital investment projects of the kind which Brazil was then building, and which CORFO had administered in Chile's past.

The world's financial and business community was delighted with the Chilean model, and it received fulsome praise from the IMF and the World Bank, being characterized in the *Wall Street Journal* as '. . . a *sane* economic experiment.' Meanwhile, the government of Chile stood by happily. After all, this was what the model was all about, private enterprise seeking money to borrow and make a profit on. If risks were being run in the process, that was not the state's responsibility, as it was involved neither as a debtor nor as a guarantor. So long as Chilean exports continued to grow, as they did throughout the years of the phoney miracle, there seemed no cause for worry. No matter that imports were growing faster even than exports, the money continued to flow, giving Chile a massive increase in its net reserves.

Some of the millions did of course find their way into productive areas, particularly to develop exports. But the bulk was used in buying up state enterprises at bargain prices, or to fuel the consumer spending spree in imported luxury goods, or to create a highly speculative land and construction boom in the upper class suburbs of Santiago.

The result was a consumer revolution. This was politically very important to the model's hopes of success, as it set out to convince Chilean workers and peasants that their experience as individual consumers was the determining factor in their lives. Even shanty-town dwellers, inadequately housed, educated, nourished and nursed, seemed to have access to the transistor radios which flooded into Chile from Taiwan and Hong Kong.

In the face of this new social reality the confidence and even the

'There will be cheap cars for everyone.'

'That's great! Now all I need is a job.'

Source: Hoy 31 January 1979

The Piranhas: Cruzat-Larrain and Javier Vial

The Pinochet decade saw an astonishing concentration of economic power within the Chilean economy, unparalleled, as one US economist was to comment, outside Somoza's Nicaragua. Two economic groups stood head and shoulders above the rest: the Cruzat-Larrain empire, and Vial's BHC group. Both were intimately linked to the Chicago Boys and through them to the government.

Neither empire existed in 1960. The core of both businesses was established in 1963, when Larrain, Claro and Vial, three friends from a private school in Santiago, bought up the shares of the *Banco Hipotecario y Fomento de Chile* (BHC), a bank so old that it was exempted from government regulation on interest rates. Using this financial loophole, and selling off BHC's property in downtown Santiago at a profit, the group grew rapidly. By 1970, it controlled the *Banco de Chile*, *Fensa* and *Mademsa* (consumer durables) COPEC (petrol stations), and some other industries, putting it among the top ten economic groups in Chile.

When Popular Unity took power, the group refused on principle to sell any shares to CORFO and its factories were 'intervened'. It retained a small factory manufacturing batteries in Arica. There was a shortage of batteries in Chile, and the group survived the Allende years by selling them on the black market.

Larrain and Claro now left the group, Larrain keeping his interest in it but leaving management to his brother-in-law, Manuel Cruzat, a Chicago economist. Vial and Cruzat together therefore ran BHC and became involved in the Monday Club. Vial was a point of contact between the Monday Club and Pablo Rodriguez, while Cruzat as an able economist was part of the original team which drew up the 1973 Chicago Plan.

After the coup, the group's 'intervened' properties were immediately returned (with the exception of the *Banco de Chile*), thus giving Vial and Cruzat a head start over competitors who had sold their shares to CORFO. In 1973, too, the group renewed its ties with the First National City Bank, giving it easy access to international credit; a second, critical advantage. When in 1975, 1976, and 1977, CORFO was auctioning off the state sector, Vial and Cruzat, who had by now split up, were in a good position to snap up key firms at bargain prices, particularly in the government subsidized area of forestry and forestry products. Throughout this period, too, the groups enjoyed a third advantage. It was a time when the economic strains of 'shock' and depression were forcing more and more businessmen into debt, and, by borrowing abroad and lending at higher rates of interest in Chile, they increased their profits and paved the way for still more acquisitions. This was the era when their

♦

voracity earned them the nickname 'the Piranhas'.

Cruzat's personal contacts with the Chicago Boys were always very close, and in the early days he was frequently consulted on details of government policy. Both he and Vial established high-powered think-tanks covering not just their own business affairs but also those of the national economy and ultimately national politics as well. The Cruzat empire in particular was a favourite stopping place for members of the government economic team after they left their posts, and for bright young Chicago Boys before they moved on to ODEPLAN. Thus Leniz, the regime's first minister of the economy, joined Cruzat to run its forestry companies. Jorge Cauas, ex-minister of finance, left the government to become head of the group's flagship, the *Banco de Santiago*. Jose Piñera left its financial company, the *Colocadora de Valores,* to enter the government first as minister of labour and then as minister of mining: the groups had a considerable interest in the privatization of the mines. As a Cruzat employee, Piñera had been editor of a house journal on the political and economic situation in Chile, outlining the basic elements for a new 'democratic' constitution which would leave ample scope for 'technical' decisions outside democratic control.

In 1978 Cruzat-Larrain controlled 37 of Chile's 250 largest companies, (worth US$937 million) and Vial controlled 25 (worth US$477 million). The privatization of Chile's social security system masterminded by Piñera, left them in control of 70 per cent of the insurance market which replaced it. The fixed exchange rate helped subsidize their debt repayments to international financial institutions. Their interests spread across all sectors of the Chilean economy: forestry, fishing, foodstuffs, wine, marketing, industry, insurance, investment companies. Javier Vial owned a weekly magazine, *Ercilla*.

But the two empires had grown through acquisitions, rather than investment and expansion of production. Both groups were indebted to such an extent that they were vulnerable to shifts in the international economy and international lending practices, not to mention the failure of Sergio de Castro's fixed exchange rate policy.

It is ironic but not untypical of the close identification between the two groups and the regime that when the crash came and the government was forced to intervene in their internal affairs, it was Vial's second-in-command at BHC, Rolf Lüders, who ordered the takeover of his *Banco de Chile*, and another old business associate, Boris Blanco, now superintendent of banks, who conducted the government's investigation. This showed that in Vial's case, debt was equivalent to about twice the banks' capital and reserves, with 54 per cent on loan to 'paper companies without genuine activities' and about two thirds unrecoverable.

triumphalism of the Chicago Boys knew no bounds. As inflation continued to fall and the economy to grow, Sergio de Castro introduced a new and controversial device which was supposed to serve the local economy as a kind of automatic regulator in line with Hayek's dream of eliminating direct government manipulation of economic affairs. This device was a fixed exchange rate and the prohibition by law of any fiscal deficit. It was argued that now the Chilean economy was so open to the international market, and so long as the government did not run a fiscal deficit, a fixed exchange rate would automatically bring Chilean inflation into line with the world rate of inflation. In June 1979, the peso was devalued 5.7 per cent and fixed at 39 pesos to the dollar. And there it remained.

The real world, however, did not quite work like a monetarist textbook. Chilean inflation did continue to fall, but it remained a little above the world inflation rate. Moreover, the dollar, to which the peso was pegged, was revalued upwards, pulling the peso with it. It should have been possible to adjust the Chilean peso to these changes. But Sergio de Castro and Bardon had staked their prestige and that of the model itself on the belief that the peso would not be devalued again. A devaluation would have had incalculable effects on the government's credibility. An even more important factor argued against future devaluation. Private foreign debt was heavily concentrated in the hands of the two major economic groups, BHC and Cruzat-Larrain (See Box Page 72). By borrowing from abroad and relending at a profit through their local banks, the *Banco de Chile*

'Archeologists have found prehistoric fossils in the south of the country.'

'*Duros* or *blandos*?'

Source: *Hoy* 17 February 1982

and the *Banco de Santiago*, these groups had financed their voracious appetite for buying up local companies and welding them into personal fiefdoms. A fixed exchange rate helped subsidize their debts.

By 1981, the accumulated effect of two years of a fixed exchange rate was an overvaluation of the peso by about 30 per cent. The result was that imports were very cheap and the prices of Chile's exports abroad expensive, which created a growing deficit in Chile's balance of trade. Theory dictated that Chile should adjust to this situation automatically, primarily through changes in the rate of interest, forcing firms and individuals to cut their demand and thus reduce their imports. The rate of interest shot up, which, combined with the existing decline in the competitiveness of Chile's exports, forced the country into a recession at the very moment when the growth in the international economy was beginning its own downward spiral, ending the inflow of foreign credit. The combination was to prove fatal.

Shadow-Boxing at Court: Duros versus Blandos

While the years of the boom continued, internal politics within the regime took a more open turn, even while the effective power of the *blandos* or Chicago Boys was seemingly sweeping all before it. During these years the *duros* or extreme nationalists supporting the government acquired a public face, if only through their columns and personal appeals to Pinochet in *La Tercera*. It was an era which was to culminate with the establishment of a *duro* think-tank, the *Centro de Estudios Nacionales* (Centre for National Studies) under the direction of Lucia Pinochet, the president's daughter. Increasingly, Pinochet's personal status as the lynchpin of the new regime and his chances of consolidating a life-long hold on power depended on the creation of at least the semblance of a political alternative to the Chicago model. This was crucial as events had marginalized the most effective real opposition to the economic team, the DINA.

The end of the DINA as a major political force began on 21 September 1976, when a car containing Allende's last minister of defence, Orlando Letelier, was blown up in Embassy Row, Washington DC. Letelier was the third potentially dangerous opponent of the government to suffer an assassination attempt. In September 1974 General Prats died in Buenos Aires, and in October 1975, the left-wing Christian Democrat leader Bernardo Leighton nearly died in the course of a similar attempt in Rome. But by 1976 the DINA had clearly over-reached itself. Letelier had powerful friends in Washington who were shocked not only by the fact of his death but by the effrontery of a foreign government sending assassins into the United States itself. A campaign for the extradiction of Manuel Contreras, judged to be the man behind this crime, began to gather steam and reached a peak in 1978.

As long as Contreras' power was intact, the Chicago reforms were potentially fragile. Traditionally, the secret police have provided a power base for Latin America's fascists, who are noted for a love of violence and enthusiasm for nationalist ideologies and nationalist economics. The DINA was more than an instrument for repression (which was to continue with very little check after the inauguration of a new secret police, the CNI). It was also a rival source of expertise within the government, employing its own economists. There was some jealousy between these *duros* and the Chicago *blandos*. In 1977 for instance, the DINA briefly tried to blacken the public image of the Chicago miracle by implicating some of the Chicago economists in a financial scandal surrounding operations in the money market. The Chicago Boys were thus undoubtedly pleased to have the DINA removed from the scene.

Pinochet's reaction must have been more ambiguous. Any increase in the DINA's power beyond a certain point would have carried the risk of it emerging from the shadows of his personal creation into an institutional power in its own right. The over-riding characteristic of the Pinochet decade was precisely his determination to eliminate all such power bases, whether civilian or in the armed forces.

All pretenders to political influence had to gain the ear of the president himself, and their influence depended in the last resort on his personal favour. That was the touchstone of Chile's military government, and it was the model for his relationship with his loyal opposition in the extreme right. As for the Chilean armed forces, they were rigorously excluded from any form of political debate, except perhaps among the small and increasingly marginal group of air force generals who surrounded General Leigh. They proved to be a hornet's nest of potential opposition which Pinochet was to attempt to clean out in 1978, during near-hostilities with Argentina.

Chile's military dictatorship was thus very different from that of the other military regimes of South America. In the latter, power rested much more clearly in the hands of the armed forces as an institution and military presidents were 'elected' by their officers for a limited term in power. There were clear rules surrounding the choice of the successor and an open debate on policies took place within the officer corps. Yet, for all the personal quality of Pinochet's dictatorship, he still required some political force to counterbalance the Chicago Boys, who were dangerously important. They were both the chief formulators of the new regime's policies and the tip of an iceberg of economic power centred around the new business empires of BHC and Cruzat-Larrain. Hence during 1978 and 1979 the anti-Chicago, anti-big business *duros* emerged as an official opposition.

Such an opposition clearly suited Pinochet. It maintained the myth that he was not personally responsible for any particular policy and thus enthroned him more securely as the incarnation of the state itself. From the *blandos'* point of view too, the effective centralization of power in Pinochet's hands avoided any further dangerous politicization of the armed forces (which would almost certainly have given the economic nationalists more weight), and allowed them to carry out their social revolution virtually unopposed.

Nevertheless, as Pinochet intended, it also gave the *blandos* a certain feeling of insecurity, not only because of the *duros'* public presence, but also because a system so wholly dependent on a single man was scarcely a firm basis for the social and economic revolution they felt mandated to carry out. The Chicago revolution had to become an intimate part of Chilean psychology and Chilean social organization. It could hardly be allowed to die with Pinochet.

Thus, during 1978 and 1979, *blando* pressure increased on Pinochet to justify his extended stay in the presidency by producing institutional reforms which would outlive his personal rule.

The Seven 'Modernizations', Beginning with Labour

These institutional reforms were the so-called 'seven modernizations', covering labour, social security, education, health, agriculture, regional policies and the judiciary. But the first and most crucial of them was a bid to institutionalize the labour market in a way favourable to the new model, while simultaneously 'liberalizing' the political climate and weaning Pinochet away from the worst excesses of repression and towards a Hayekian 'Constitution of Liberty' as a model of political control.

The opportunity came in 1978 when contacts between the AFL-CIO and the Group of Ten Christian Democrat trade union leaders finally produced a US threat to boycott Chile's goods. At the same time unrest in the copper mines resulted in the third strike or threatened strike in as many years, this time in Chuquicamata. Reluctantly, the president agreed to introduce a new Labour Code and pave the way for a normalization of trade union activities. However, this was only done after steps were taken to ensure that no dangerous consequences would follow. A marked stiffening in the penalties for 'claiming to be a union representative without legal title' was introduced and in October 1978 the seven union federations which supported the left-wing CNS were dissolved.

Lessons of Madeco. We have to be prepared

Workers at Madeco began the process of collective bargaining sure that they would not make any substantial gains in wages but that at least they could recover some of their lost purchasing power by gaining a rise in line with inflation. After a 57 day strike they were forced back to work on the same basis as when the strike began with 62 comrades dismissed and more than 100 who abandoned the struggle along the route. (Of 354 who went on strike at the beginning, 130 went back to work at the firm's invitation after 30 days.)

Drawing a balance sheet of these events, one would expect to find an abandoned union, perhaps with a few officials, going through the motions. The reality is different. Here in Madeco there is bustling activity, and several lessons have been learned.

The strike being finished, all those who took part in it and who didn't 'return with their tails between their legs' head for the union centre once their shift is over. They talk and raise the spirits of their dismissed mates, who have formed a committee to defend the source of their work. A few play ping-pong, others prepare a meal for the night, hoping to make rations meet demand a bit better as 'we were short' over lunch. The biggest group sits with those who were dismissed.

Leaders apart, no one wants his name reported, for fear of reprisals. What they say, first of all, is that workers cannot negotiate their wages on the basis of the present labour laws. 'There's no point, not for us. It suits the employer, especially if they have stock to get rid of or people they want to dismiss.'

They are most impressed with the solidarity shown by the rest of the trade union movement. A solidarity which allowed them to feed around 350 families through *ollas comunes*, to pay their gas and electricity bills, and to give out family packets.

But they talk about another kind of solidarity which has not been seen in this country in ten years: 'We lacked concrete support from the other organizations, like protest strikes and demonstrations, the way we used to have them before', says a young worker.

On this improvised balance sheet the workers are drawing up, fear plays an important part. 'As the labour laws allow the firm to employ new workers during the strike, Madeco put out an advertisement and more than 7,000 people turned up. We went to tell them that they shouldn't break this strike, and 84 of us ended up in the police station, on their books and treated like criminals.'

They all agree that this was the point when the strike lost its momentum. Some people stopped coming to the union centre, and several 'turned tail' and returned to work.

Fear was obvious after a month on strike; still, the workers took a vote and decided to continue their protest. They decided by a clear majority to do it, 'but it was never the same.' 'Before and during the strike, the firm tried to undermine it by calling it political and saying that not all of us could go back. That put the wind up those who found any pretext for turning tail.'

'Turning tail' is a grave crime among workers. All those who committed this crime (going back to work before the strike ended) 'we've surrounded with walls of ice'. They don't speak to them. They don't sit with them in the canteen. 'They avoid us themselves because they must be ashamed. They lost everything, just like us. Some of them have been dismissed, and have turned up at the union and we can't throw them out, but the rest of the comrades complain. It's a problem we'll have to discuss in a full meeting because we can't leave them without support either.'

And here's another of the weaknesses of the Madeco strike. Not all workers showed the same degree of understanding of what was going on. 'The fact that almost 130 people turned tail shows it. If you heard their excuses: "Old man, my gas has run out". "Don't worry, we'll find you enough money to pay for it". And that night you'd take them the thousand pesos to buy a gas cylinder and have a little over for bread. And the next day the same worker would come in with his thousand pesos, saying it was better to go back to work. They couldn't stand the situation any longer,' says Carlos Vargas, one of the strike leaders.

'Most of them are young people who have no experience of trade union struggles, of how unions have had to fight for their rights,' said one of the leaders of those who have now been dismissed.

He thinks that workers and strike leaders should all be given a training course in how to manage a struggle. In Madeco's case, he explains, they began to make preparations too late in the day. 'After one round of collective bargaining, the union should begin to prepare for the next one immediately, getting money together, tins of food, school books and pens for the children. Be prepared.'

Carlos Vargas says that now all workers are voluntarily giving 200 pesos a month to help those who were dismissed and a part of this is going towards a fund for the next round of collective bargaining.

Solidaridad April 1983.

The new Chicago Boy, José Piñera, took over at the ministry of labour in January 1979. He believed that Chile's old, bad, politicized labour movement had emerged as a consequence of an economic model which had given governments enormous powers over the factors which determine an employer's profit margins and which had granted trade unions significant economic advantages. In this he was of course a diligent student of Hayek, as the populist appeals to those exploited by organized labour clearly showed: '. . . consumers, pensioners, the unemployed, those at work who cannot form trade unions . . .'

While the *duros* were arguing for the state to impose a loyal trade union movement on Chile's subversive rank-and-file workers, Piñera argued for free union elections. Remove the state's direct influence over collective bargaining, he said, and Chile's trade union leaders will cease to be interested in politics, because it would bring them no economic advantage. He also argued however, that it might take one or two bad experiences with the new laws before the rank-and-file learned their lesson!

Because Piñera was a student of Hayek's, trade unionists also had to learn the lesson that they could not interfere in the free workings of the labour market. The new Labour Code set out therefore to strip them of their 'monopoly powers', by devising a legal framework which weakened the trade unions as much as possible. Thus the union movement was fragmented at factory level, with different negotiations being timetabled to ensure that no two factories in the same sector would acquire 'monopoly powers' by negotiating together. Employers had the right to postpone the date of negotiations if they fell at a time when a strike would be particularly damaging. Strikes were legally limited to 60 days, after which strikers were formally dismissed.

No possibility existed in the new legislation for any genuine 'collective contract', in the sense that the union could only negotiate for the series of individuals who signed their name to the agreement, and had no powers whatsoever to fix a future rate for the job. With previous legislation protecting workers from arbitrary dismissal now almost a dead letter, the Chicago reforms intended 'to make the labour market more flexible'. Trade unions which tried to impose wages above their members' market value were open to abrupt dismissal, even if the contract was signed.

In all these measures, Piñera was presumably remembering Hayek's dictum that economic liberty, the free operation of the market, is more fundamental than any other liberty. He may also have been influenced by Hayek's belief that the state does not intervene in individual affairs if it does no more than lay down ground rules, setting up an automatic system in which individuals are free to operate, so long as they obey these guidelines. Chile's workers were not such subtle philosophers. They drew the obvious conclusion, that the new Labour Plan was a massive state intervention in union affairs designed to favour employers at the workers' expense.

Nonetheless, the introduction of collective bargaining in 1979 and

1980 for the first time since the coup was enormously important to Chile's labour movement, and not just in economic terms. Piñera had hoped that the new union elections would remove opposition organizations such as the Group of Ten and the CNS permanently from the scene. He believed the elections would show that there was no support from the rank-and-file for their 'politicized' activities. That was hardly the actual result. In the state sector, where the size and small number of plants allowed for some rough-and-ready calculations of political loyalty, the opposition seems to have won the elections handsomely, particularly in the critically important copper mines of Chuquicamata and El Salvador. The most decisive effect of the new law was to weaken even more obviously the claims of the junta's favourite trade union leaders to represent their rank-and-file, as the *Secretario de los Gremios* candidate came bottom of the poll in the Huachipato steel plant.

Nevertheless, the opposition labour movement of 1978 was a paper tiger, in spite of its courage and its international support. Essentially, it was the creation of union leaders from another era whose luck or politics had enabled them to survive the coup. New activity on the shop floor brought with it a new generation of leaders, giving expression to their members' feelings of frustration and a significant demand, not just for some restoration of their economic losses, but also for recognition of their human dignity. 1980 was the year when textile workers began a series of 59 day strikes against the social order which had treated them so badly. It was also the year when junta supporter Bernardino Castillo retired from the Copper Workers' Confederation (CTC), to make way for younger men with very different political views. That such things could happen again in Chile was an enormous step forward for the opposition as a whole.

Pinochet himself clearly drew this conclusion. The relative freedom from repression which Chile had enjoyed in 1979 drew abruptly to a close in time for May Day 1980, and was not to return. Piñera's attempt to replace repression with an 'automatic' system of economic controls, largely using the existing high levels of unemployment, was thus unceremoniously put in abeyance.

The new constitution published in 1980 provided the president with even tougher powers under 'states of emergency' in which normal civil rights could be suspended. Once it was introduced in March 1981, a new era of murders by the security forces was to begin, though this time instead of disappearing, the corpses were increasingly to appear as charred fragments in burnt-out cars, supposedly wrecked in the course of shoot-outs between extremists and the security forces.

The 'modernizations' in the other six areas had a less resounding impact. Chile's social security system was restructured, essentially as a private activity run by Chile's financiers, with minimum state guarantees. Not only was it much cheaper for employers (and apparently for workers as well, since they paid less in contributions), but the massive funds, previously used to cut state deficits or to bolster the private consumption of the better-off workers, now went directly to the business empires BHC and Cruzat-Larrain. Education was also broken up, with the state system being farmed out to the municipalities, presumably now to compete with one another for a better service. Apart from twelve specially designated 'professsions', law, accounting, architecture, some sciences and of course economics, the university campuses were stripped of their exclusive right to provide degree level courses. Anyone in Santiago could now offer to teach sociology, providing someone was willing to pay for it.

None of these reforms raised really significant protests, though right and left wings of the organized labour movement were worried by the apparent dependence of workers' social security on the fragile futures of private enterprise. Still, signs of a conflict between the Chicago Boys and Chile's 'professions', those private monopolies accustomed to overcharging the public for their services, were already on the horizon. The first battleground came in journalism, which lost its special school at the University of Chile and its title to be a professional career. The second, more significant, battle came with the doctors, over reforms to Chile's national health service.

Doctors themselves had supported the breaking up of the service after the coup, and its replacement by private services which they saw as being run by doctors, with the state providing the finances for health services to the poor. Under such a system decisions would still have been made by the professionals, and need would still have been the final criterion for supply. The Chicago Boys were not interested in such a scheme for privatization, ignoring as it did the profit motive. They wanted health care to be handed over directly to private business, with doctors acting essentially as employees. To prove that private enterprise could run a hospital more cheaply and more efficiently than the state, they staged a demonstration. They sold the modern hospital in Santiago, *Paula Jaraquemada*, to an American multinational, and set out plans for breaking up the national health service into regional units competing with one another, with the aim of making a private sector model feasible for Chile as a whole.

The first effective resistance to this plan came from newly graduated medical students. They were unable to find jobs, and thus secure a full medical qualification, in a system in which employment in the government-run health service was contracting. Working conditions and pay for this group were highly exploitative, and their need of a year's practice in order to qualify made them easy prey for

82

private clinics looking for labour on the cheap. In 1980, the students occupied the offices of their own professional association, the *Colegio Medico*. The doctors, especially the younger ones, argued that without internal elections the *Colegio* no longer represented their interests. The students demands were for free professional elections, and the protection and expansion of the old national health service to provide them with jobs. It was the first real protest of the middle classes against the regime.

Most doctors were disturbed by the new health proposals. The idea that private demand should determine supply posed a threat to Chile's public health traditions, of which they were justifiably proud. The doctors rallied against the new Health Plan, and Pinochet wisely retreated. The Health Plan was subsequently modified. The national health service however continued to be grossly underfinanced, given the fact that health was not a priority in the overall Chicago model, and its patients were forced to pay even for emergency services.

Security: (Latin *Securitis*.) 'Confidence, state of personal tranquillity due to freedom from fear.'

'How strange! Must be a bad dictionary.'

Source: Hoy 8 July 1981

Pinochet: The Embodiment of a 'Constitution of Liberty'

Once the economic miracle seemed assured, pressures also built up to give the regime a constitution. This would mend Chile's severely damaged international reputation, legitimize the regime internally, and provide a framework for controlling political debate. The Chicago Boys' ideal would have been an 'automatic' political system, requiring no human intervention to run it and thus leaving no room for political manipulation to serve the interests of some particular sector. But politics is a cornerstone of Chilean social life. By 1979 even Chile's right were showing an eagerness to re-establish some kind of political forum. From their fashionable *soirées*, where the National Party slowly re-emerged, through the ambitious Christian Democrat 'multiparty' Group of 24, to the Church's *Academia de Humanismo Cristiano* (Academy of Christian Humanism), every shade of political opinion established its own think-tank to analyse and debate the political situation.

At Leigh's instigation, a constitutional committee had been set up in the first week after the coup. Pinochet however had largely ignored it, until in 1976 he established the Council of State. In July 1977 he made an important speech outlining the steps to be taken towards institutionalization, but without consulting Leigh. In August 1977 Leigh began to publicize his own views on the new constitution. Having long since abandoned the corporatist ideas with which he had flirted in the first few months after the coup, he now came out in favour of a return to a parliamentary democracy in which all parties but the Marxists were included, a model of Chile's future regime which he shared with Frei's wing of the Christian Democrats. Furthermore, he called for a strict timetable. Leigh, perhaps more than anyone else in Chile, was already well aware that Pinochet intended to stay in power until the day he died.

In July 1978, as the *blandos* were attempting to restore Chile's international reputation and end its diplomatic isolation, Pinochet asked for Leigh's resignation from the junta. The dangers of any opposition from within the armed forces were minimal, not only because the air force had long since become a marginal factor in their internal politics, but also because Chile was facing a threat of war from Argentina in the south over the disputed islands in the Beagle Channel, recently awarded to Chile by a British team of mediators. It was indicative of Pinochet's character that, even so, he indirectly asked Leigh if the air force would mutiny, and despite Leigh's assurances that it would not, surrounded the air force's barracks with troops and tanks.

Eight air force generals tendered their resignation together with

Leigh. General Matthei became head of the air force and a member of the junta. Even with Pinochet's personal choice at its head, however, the air force continued to be a mild voice of criticism within the junta. Leigh himself stayed in Chile, showing a certain amount of personal courage in view of the fate of Pinochet's other potential opponents. He was hoping perhaps to re-emerge as a focus of opposition if a crisis developed.

In this fashion, Chile took the decisive step towards its so-called 'Constitution of Liberty', the name, if nothing else, taken from Hayek's *magnum opus* of political philosophy. In fact the prestige of the *blandos* as political thinkers had begun to wane somewhat within the government. This followed the failure of a premature attempt by Hernan Cubillos to bring Chile's diplomatic isolation to an end with an official visit by Pinochet himself to the Philippines. The visit was a disaster as the authoritarian Philippines' dictator President Marcos delivered a public snub to Pinochet, presumably as a result of American influence. Cubillos was dismissed.

The constitution, when it came, proved to be a decisive reinforcement of Pinochet's personal power and his freedom to resort to the arbitrary repression of dissidents. It was also the work of a cabal of right-wing lawyers whose objective was to preserve Chile's free market economy from any political challenge. The power of a free people to determine its own future was drastically curtailed by confining political discussion and activities within strictly defined limits. Journalists who raised issues in a fashion which the government regarded as 'subversive' faced professional disqualification. It was not surprising that Chile's new ruler, as no other before him, was highly conscious of the political power of the media. The activities of the parties were similarly restricted, with Marxist parties banned outright. Elections to a congress were to come in 1990 and until the new law on political parties came into force, political activity was illegal. Furthermore, the new law would determine the details of the internal organization of the new parties, and would proscribe any activities that were not regulated by the law. The armed forces had an effective veto of all political developments through a new Council of National Security, which joined congress, the executive and the judiciary as one of the key institutions of the state.

The new constitution was tailored to ensure that Pinochet himself would remain in power. A transitional period of eight years was proposed before it came into effect (taking the country to March 1989), during which time Pinochet would act as Chile's legal president. Thereafter, the power to name the country's first constitutional president would lie with the military junta. It would undoubtedly

The Chilean 'Constitution of Liberty'

The plebiscite of 11 September 1980 approved a new constitution intended to enshrine the main principles of the two ideologies to which the Pinochet regime was simultaneously committed, National Security and *laissez-faire*, in a way which would protect both of them from any future democratic decision by the Chilean people.

The name given to the new constitution was a deliberate plagiarism from Friedrich Von Hayek's famous work of political philosophy, *The Constitution of Liberty*. Hayek has argued consistently that the preservation of economic freedom is logically and philosophically more important than the preservation of the institutions of democracy, suggesting that 'democracy can acquire totalitarian powers' and that 'an authoritarian government can act according to liberal principles.' As an internationally prestigious thinker on issues related to the limitation of democratic freedom and an apologist for authoritarianism, the views of Hayek were given pride of place.

However, the new constitution did not give Chile's *laissez-faire* exponents, the *blandos*, guarantees that the state would stop its intervention in the economy. Although the *blandos* gained constitutional guarantees of the right to a private educational system and a private health system, the state's commitment to maintain public services in these areas was maintained. The *blandos* also gained 'freedom from trade union coercion' through a constitutional ban on the closed shop and a constitutional prohibition on any union activities outside Chile's highly restrictive legal framework, with heavy penalties for disobedience. But they failed to gain a constitutional prohibition against any form of fiscal deficit, or a constitutional status for the central bank independent of interference from the executive.

Chile's nationalists (the *duros*) gained a conception of sovereignty vested not in its people but in 'the nation' as an abstract concept. They gained a National Security Council with veto powers on any political questions which it felt infringed the field of national security. The council was controlled by the commanders-in-chief of the armed forces, who, once appointed, no president could remove. The *duros* also gained the total disenfranchisement of any Chilean publicly espousing ideas of class conflict or violence, or the dissolution of the family; finally, they gained the right for the government and the law courts to have final decision over any method of organizing a political party, and any views it might express.

Both sides gained a limited democracy, in which the executive had ample powers of decision and the people a very limited framework for choice. The president, for instance, had the right to appoint 25

▶

per cent of the senate's members and with the support of just three of its elected members out of 26, he could block many important pieces of legislation. Also the faculty of deciding on what basis senate and congress were to be elected remained with the president. Anyone opposing these views or expressing totalitarian ideologies was liable to disenfranchisement for ten years at a first offence, with increased penalties for repeating the offence. Meanwhile, the president's arbitrary powers were firmly entrenched. He could not only decide what laws should be passed, but also invoke a new 'state of siege' at any time, in which all civil rights would be automatically suspended.

name Pinochet and he would serve, like all Chile's future presidents, for an eight-year term, an extension of the old six-year term provided for by the 1925 constitution. But unlike all future Chilean presidents, Pinochet would be personally allowed a second successive term in office. Thus the new constitution guaranteed Chile 24 years of Pinochet in power, a one-man dictatorship until 1997.

8 The Roots of Resistance

The Growth of Opposition

There is some continuity between the present opposition and the final months of 1973. In a sense, resistance to the Pinochet regime began with Allende's dramatic stance, machine gun in hand, at the Moneda Palace. Human rights organizations can look back on the pioneer activities of the original ecumenical *Comité Pro Paz*, though there are now half-a-dozen committees representing relatives of the disappeared, the executed, the political prisoners and those in exile, as well as the *Vicaría de Solidaridad* itself. The seven trade union federations which finally came together to form the CNS with a public protest in 1976, had survived during the period of massive repression thanks to left-wing activists. They determined that Chile's trade union organizations should not disappear at the national level as they seemed likely to do at the level of individual firms. This struggle had already achieved some basic success by the time the ILO mission arrived in November 1974.

There is another sense, however, in which the present opposition effectively dates from the era of 'shock', and is closely linked with the decision of the Catholic Church during this period to shelter opposition tendencies of almost all political shades, including Marxists. In one fashion or another, the *Vicaría de Solidaridad* has given a helping hand to most of the forms of popular protest we describe below. This broader opposition, protected by the church, draws together Marxists and Christian Democrats. It has always been riven by the political ambiguities inherent in Christian Democracy. Some members of the party were willing to join forces with the Marxists for similar social goals, like Manuel Bustos, president of the

CNS. Others would sacrifice such unity in exchange for US financial and political support, like Eduardo Rios, of the old Group of Ten, which had become the Democratic Workers Union (UDT). Still others have continued to support an 'anti-communist' coup and the government which came from it, though these have been a dwindling minority over the years.

The roots of the present Chilean opposition as a political force with mass support lie in the brief period of liberalization which accompanied the seven modernizations and the 1980 plebiscite on the Constitution of Liberty. It is not the creation of any single political party, nor even of all the country's political parties put together, but a dense tangle of intertwined social networks strengthened and given national impetus by explicitly political and party ties. It is in fact a very Chilean phenomenon, with its origins in patterns of social organization dating back nearly a hundred years, and living proof of the failure of the 'Chicago revolution' to eradicate politics from Chilean life.

Community-level organizations such as the Neighbourhood Committees, Popular Supply Committees and Mothers' Centres typical of Chile's shanty-towns before 1973 were largely destroyed by the coup. They began to function again in 1975, during 'shock', when the *Vicaría de Solidaridad* encouraged local groups to set up children's canteens *(comedores infantiles)* and unemployed workers' centres *(bolsas de cesantes)*, providing some money and basic foods. This was also the period when the Christian base communities *(Comunidades Cristianos de Base)* of the Catholic Church began to operate. They were inevitably regarded as subversive by the government, and subject to the repression which re-appeared in 1976.

The Labour Code stiffened such organizations by facilitating contacts with workers in local factories, through the support and solidarity which these outsiders (often with the encouragement of the zonal *vicaría*) were able to offer to those on strike. Collections of money and food were taken for the common kitchens or *ollas communes* (literally 'common pots'), a crucial element in Chilean labour movement traditions which revived under the strikes made legal by the new labour legislation. (See Box Page 90). The experiences in collective bargaining under the prevailing harsh conditions in turn educated a new generation of trade union activists at plant level in the necessity for broader solidarity with their own struggles, and turned them outwards towards sympathetic organizations in the community. When, for instance, the small southern textile town of Penco was badly hit by factory closures, it

Ollas comunes: a little here, a little there

The idea was to get them together to talk. Not about the weather or football, but about how they 'fill the pot'. So it was that on 29 April, representatives of eleven of the twenty-three *ollas comunes* presently operating in the eastern zone met at the invitation of the *vicaría* of the east.

'. . . The mothers collected papers from house to house and sell them. This gives us a little finance for the common pot. Then every one brings a little rice, macaroni, semolina or corn. That's how we prepare lunch. We beg for vegetables in the market. Some of the stall owners give it to us with good grace, some with a curse, but they give it to us . . .' A woman from Puente Alto with six children tells the story. Her husband has been unemployed for a year. The *olla* to which she belongs feeds a hundred people, men, women, old people, children.

'Our *olla* feeds a hundred and seventy people. The Christian Community runs it and brings the food. We have only modest resources, but at least we're providing food for those who now have nothing to eat,' says another woman from Nunoa.

'We're from La Florida. We have 122 families in the *olla comun*. We go to the sawmills to get sawdust for a fire, and in the afternoons we collect round the local businesses. We also get help from the *vicaría*. We have to struggle to keep these 122 families going. Many of the children are suffering from malnutrition. We must get things moving and give them a future,' says another shanty-town woman.

3600 people are eating at the *ollas comunes* which function in the camps and shanty-towns of various municipalities in the eastern sector of Santiago. The number has grown as the population's living conditions have got worse.

The shanty-town dwellers are beginning to overcome their fears — for many local mayors look askance at the *ollas* and in some cases, people organizing them have been arrested, and are coming together to ensure a minimum ration of food every day. When resources are very scarce, they manage at least a weekly bean pot.

In the Lo Hermida area of Nuñoa, where the floods of last year created a real disaster zone, the emergency stimulated a number of *ollas comunes*. Nine of these are still functioning, grouped together in a *coordinadora*. As one leader explains, uniting fòrces has allowed them to buy some products more cheaply, such as beans, squash, and soup bones.

'We have a plan to build a bakery serving all the *ollas*. All those who are organized will be able to eat bread. Affiliated *ollas* will have the right to send it five workers every month, who will be paid for their work.'

Putting peso with peso, they have bought some machines. Just now they are collecting money to buy the oven and a plot of land to install it on.

The organizers of this first meeting of eastern area *ollas comunes* were pleased with the results.

'It was useful because those with more initiative and creativity told those who were just beginning about their experiences, explaining to people who perhaps are still very dependent on us for help, when this is only a supplement which could come to an end in the future,' reported Ana Maria Medioli, a social worker.

Vicar Cristian Precht pointed out that the church's intention was 'to support the ways the people organize themselves. The ability to unite forces is the great strength of poor people. It is this which has allowed them to overcome such immense troubles in recent times.'

'I know that some people are troubled by the organization of the poor, and look on it with a great deal of wariness. But it is the best resource they have, their only non-violent weapon, and that is why we support it,' he emphasized.

Solidaridad May 1983.

---

was the local ceramics factory *Fanaloza* which organized a conference on unemployment in the area, inviting the unemployed, representatives of other local unions, and the Church.

As conditions in Chile began to worsen in 1982 and 1983, such local organizations multiplied, adding committees of the homeless to their ranks and new organizations of the unemployed, often set up by factory workers stimulated by the experience of the Labour Code, even if they lost their jobs in its wake. (See Box Page 78). Thus the *comedores infantiles* organized by the Church during 'shock' were replaced by *ollas comunes* meeting the needs of entire families, coping with the effects of economic failure on a group of families where male unemployment might reach 80 per cent.

Trade unions are the traditional backbone of Chile's protest movements. Immediately after the coup they were immobilized, stripped of their activists at factory level and of the most 'politicized' members of the rank and file. By law, vacancies in plant level leadership were filled by the oldest employees, resulting in the geriatrification of trade union representation. Collective bargaining was suspended, and all union meetings had to be notified to the police 48 hours in advance. Where local unions survived as functioning organizations, they did so because 'shock' forced whole factories into a struggle against closure, or because the old union had an independent social centre which could function as a focus for organization, as in the copper mine at El Salvador.

Between 1974 and 1978, trade unionism in Chile became synonymous with the 'old hands' who were its national representatives campaigning through public petitions to the government on unemployment, wages, conditions, and trade union rights. These 'old hands' showed enormous personal courage, as the fate of Tucapel Jimenez, assassinated in 1982, helps remind us (See Box Page 93). Ominous telephone calls and shadowy figures in civilian cars keeping close watch over them were part of their normal routine. Among those associated with the CNS, Bustos, Guzman, and Hector Cuevas all spent many months in jail, and all had friends and colleagues who 'disappeared'.

Still, these men reflected a world of party loyalties and sectarian divisions frozen in 1973. Every public trade union figure depended on support from international trade union interests for his personal security. These international organizations had their own political interests, not necessarily suited to Chile's needs. This was the period when the CNS and the Group of Ten were formed, the former representing broadly socialist and left-wing christian tendencies dependent on European Social Democrat and Eastern Socialist support, the latter very closely tied to the United States AFL-CIO. CLAT, the Latin American regional federation of Catholic unions, had similar ties with the United Workers Front (FUT). The government reacted by recruiting its own trade union leaders from among those it had confirmed in office after the coup and formed the National Union of Chilean Workers (UNTRACH).

The Labour Code took this trade unionism into a new phase, by allowing the election of a new generation of trade union leaders at plant level, and, still more vital, rank and file discussion within the plant over what they should or should not do. New figures such as Oscar Piño of the Goodyear factory emerged to organize rank and file fronts of Santiago workers to stand against the threat of unemployment, though, like Piño himself, they were often the first victims of dismissals under the new, management-oriented Labour Code. Gradually, this movement of renovation led to the removal of the conservative, ex-Christian Democrat leadership of the copper workers (Bernardino Castillo, a key figure in UNTRACH) and put in a new, aggressive leadership elected by the copper workers in conference. These men were prepared to consider organizing a general strike in defence of union rights, as they were to do in 1982.

By 1982 in fact, however hobbled its collective bargaining might have been, Chile's trade union movement was once again functioning

Death of a Trade Union Leader

Tucapel Jimenez, 60 years old, married, was found murdered on Thursday 25 February 1982, about 7 p.m., in the road to Lampa near El Peralillo Bridge. According to his relatives and the police, his body was in the front of his car, a Datsun taxi. It was leaning to the right, and had very deep wounds made with some kind of knife at the side of the neck. A policeman said to the family, 'They tried to cut his head off, but it must have been for revenge because there's almost no blood in the car. They killed him somewhere else.'

Jimenez, a trade union leader, had emerged at the head of a possible united movement of workers against the difficult economic situation and the loss of their rights. He left his home at 9.20 that morning, and at 10 o'clock, was due to have a meeting with Manuel Bustos, President of the CNS. The last person to speak to him was the owner of a newspaper kiosk near his home.

Tucapel Jimenez was permanently followed by a car. 'It doesn't mean anything to me anymore,' he told neighbour and fellow-activist Carlos Santa Maria, President of the Association of Assistant Social Security Officers. 'At first he would wait for me to get home, and then we would go into his house together . . .' an elementary security precaution which Jimenez soon ceased to bother with, just as he ignored the threatening telephone calls which only ended on the day of his death.

He wasn't frightened either by the attack on his union's headquarters on 7 January 1977, when unknown persons, never located, tried to burn down the union offices and left organizer Milenko Mihovilocic with wounds which put him in hospital. Workers, union leaders and personalities such as Generals (retired) Gustavo Leigh and Nicanor Diaz Estrada, who came to the crematorium, were agreed that this was 'a political crime', which took place at a crucial moment (when unity had almost been achieved) and was directed at the key man, one who was respected by all sectors and all political tendencies.

. . . A police source told *Solidaridad* that as for ordinary criminal motives, 'We've ruled them out. It could be left-wing extremists, and if it is, we'll find them. But if it's the madmen of the extreme right, sicker than the others, we'll only get so far and then the trail will end.'

Solidaridad March 1982

as a mass movement, less amenable to control by the government or by its international benefactors, less easily replaced by the public fiction of an official union movement loyally devoted to the president of Chile. Equally important, the process of popular organization, which could provide an important network of support during strikes, gave a new sense of morale even to those who were the victims of the Labour Code and lost their jobs after a strike had ended.

Culture is enormously important to Chile's popular organizations, perhaps above all through the medium of folk-song where figures like Violeta Parra and Victor Jara (murdered in 1973) were political symbols for an entire generation. After the coup, left-wing songs and the folk tradition out of which they had grown were banned. Protest art re-emerged into the public eye first of all through the more respectable medium of the theatre, where plays about unemployment such as The Three Marias *(Las Tres Marías)* were beginning to be produced by 1978. The following year, new folk clubs or *peñas* were being set up with a paying clientele to foster folk artists who would then, unpaid, take their art out to workers on strike and to the multiplicity of popular organizations in the shanty-towns. The revival of a student culture dominated by the opposition undoubtedly gave these new revivals of an old Chilean tradition an added boost; so too did the various opposition parties, determined patrons in their own right. The government attempted to solve the problem by repression, going so far in 1980 as to arrest a number of students attending a *peña* and send them into internal exile. But the new folk song, like its predecessor, survived.

Party networks also survived, emerging in full strength and with a remarkable degree of unity during the campaign against the new constitution. None of Chile's left-wing factions actually disappeared as a result of repression and exile. Rather, they multiplied; the strains of change and international pressures bred a process of fragmentation which ultimately only a return to democracy will cure. Although very small, many did have some ties with the factories and shanty-towns. They preserved an existence based on bulletins for those in Chile and for those in exile, on the organization of national and international conferences, on encounters and 'convergences' between various groups in sympathy with one another, and on hard political work. Without the efforts of party activists, much of that non-political human rights and trade union opposition to the government which began to emerge in 1976 and 1977, and slowly flowered in 1979 and 1980, would not have had the same international effect.

By 1980, Socialist and Communist Party leaflets were once again making an appearance on the doorsteps of the uncommitted, and in Santiago's shanty-towns.

Estimates of the left's political support during this period are mostly speculative. At one time there were eight socialist parties in existence, and three MAPUs (See Chile: In Brief). Even in 1983, as the opposition campaign against the government gathered speed, three factions of the Socialist Party still had to put separate signatures to the creation of a multi-party alliance against the government.

The Communist Party has also suffered internal tensions, as the strains of an alliance between local activists and party members in exile took their toll. In 1981, after the excitement of the campaign against the constitution had waned, and with no immediate alternative in sight, the party decided to give its backing to armed opposition against the dictatorship, effectively forming an alliance with the MIR which would have horrified its membership a decade earlier. However, such a strategy made little sense to many of the party's trade union leaders in Chile. They were attempting to operate publicly within a rigid legal framework, at risk from all sides, and working in conditions where an alliance with left-wing Christian Democrats was a matter of survival and the search for some kind of united front of the whole labour movement the single most important political task.

With some help from international funds, the opposition set up a variety of think-tanks, sometimes tied to particular parties, as in the case of CIEPLAN, representing a sector of Christian Democracy. It was more usual, in the case of the left, for two or three different factions with broadly similar outlooks to unite, occasionally bringing together a broad swathe of opinion, as in the Group of Twenty-Four which took advantage of the 1980 plebiscite to present its own report on changes required to the 1925 constitution, or in the *Academia de Humanismo Cristiano* organized by the church. Gradually, the opposition's analysis of contemporary Chilean reality emerged from the simple caricature of the new regime as 'fascist' and came to grips with the ideological complexities of 'the Chicago revolution' and the prospects for the country under the new economic order. Sketches of future alternatives were drawn up, ranging from a right-wing, Christian Democrat 'Chicago' model with a 'human face', to more radical projections of an increased role for the Chilean state in a new economy. But as a gathering world financial crisis destabilized the Chilean economy along with other economies on the continent, individual national solutions for small countries like Chile looked increasingly less feasible.

The Christian Democrat Party would play a pivotal role in any future Chile without Pinochet. Frei's death in 1982 and the election of Gabriel Valdes to replace him shifted the party to the left again, committing it to more mobilization and direct confrontation with the government. An alliance with the left seemed the logical next step.

It was hindered by two developments: the Communist Party's own immediate commitment to armed opposition was impossible to square with Christian Democracy's US connections; and the re-emergence of a democratic opposition much further to the right. The National Party, which had so willingly dissolved itself in 1973, now came back into political life as an independent force critical of the government, looking for allies, with its own think-tank to prepare the road for a democratic future. Its re-appearance offered the more right-wing, pro-US elements in Christian Democracy a chance to turn Chile towards a 'guided democracy', particularly if the armed forces retained their own cohesion during the transfer of power, and wished to play a key role in any political changes. After all, the National Party and the Christian Democrats had formed the original alliance to bring down Allende's government, a mere ten years previously.

So by 1983, Chile's political parties had re-established themselves firmly on the political scene. The ten years of the Pinochet government had failed to eliminate them as a vital force in Chile's political life. Together with an increasingly militant mass movement they were seeking to shape a future for Chile without Pinochet. However, the unknown factor was when, in what circumstances, and with what final degree of mass involvement, Pinochet would fall.

9 The End of the Dream

Rude Awakening

Public discontent with the Pinochet regime had its roots in the era of the model's greatest apparent success. What was true of workers in trade unions and political activists was, *mutatis mutandi*, also true for individual doctors, journalists, small farmers unable to cope with a free market policy in agriculture, and retailers upset by the competition from the swollen informal sector of street-sellers driven out of jobs elsewhere. Slowly all of them began to articulate their grievances alongside those of organized labour. In spite of the fact that sections of these groups had always been overtly 'loyalist', the *gremio* movement of opposition was being reborn alongside a new labour movement. This time however, *El Mercurio* was not organizing it, nor was it receiving finance from abroad.

The brief, sunny days of liberalization which were already clouding over in the early part of 1980, nevertheless gave Chile the first taste since the coup of an open political opposition seeking mass support. During the referendum campaign on the new constitution, public meetings were held and demonstrations organized. It was the Christian Democrats who led opposition to the new proposals, enjoying as they did a semi-legal status and the protection of powerful international allies, but the campaign was a united effort drawing on the forces of all Chile's left-wing parties as well. Essential contacts for the future were made.

Some public impact was achieved — enough to spark a movement among sectors of the old National Party towards a position more openly independent of the dictatorship. Every general in the armed

97

forces was supplied with a copy of Fernando Dahse's survey of the new business empires, *The Map of Extreme Wealth*. This touched a sore nerve, for in Chile, unlike Brazil and Argentina, the generals had not been absorbed into the new financial elite.

'We're celebrating 100 years since Keynes was born.'

'I'm not celebrating, I'm missing him.'

Source: Hoy 1 July 1981

The Economic Collapse

In 1980, as these tensions began to emerge, inflation and unemployment were still falling. The electoral victories of Margaret Thatcher in Britain and Ronald Reagan in the United States assured the Chicago Boys of international support, and confirmed their heady optimism. Confidence was high in Chile, where there was a construction boom in luxury houses, flats and offices in Santiago, and the president was building himself a new luxurious presidential palace. Even the fixed exchange rate seemed a success, and the president of the central bank confidently predicted that it would remain fixed 'for many years'.

Cracks in the miracle were soon to appear. The world recession hit the price of copper and other minerals. Chile's trade deficit grew as the fixed exchange rate forced up the price of its agricultural exports on contracting international markets. In the Chicago model, if there is an international recession, the adjustment of the Chilean economy, like that of other economies, is meant to be 'automatic', operating through the invisible hand of the market. The problem is that what may be merely a cold to a large economy like the United States, whose

> PERO... A MÍ
> ME DIJERON QUE
> LA SOLUCIÓN ERA
> ENDEUDARSE

'But . . . they told me the solution was to borrow more.'

Source: Hoy 22 July 1981

economic vitality is based on a wide spread of different activities, can easily become a case of pneumonia for a small, open economy like Chile, particularly as the Chicago policies had removed all local immunities to the disease.

May 1981 saw the collapse of the sugar monopoly CRAV *(Companía Refinería de Azúcar de Viña del Mar)*, flagship of Jorge Ross's business empire (one of the Monday Club's original members). It should have been a warning, but the arrogance of the Chicago Boys was such that they shrugged it aside and declared there would be no change in the government's policies. Incredibly, for a short period, foreign bankers agreed and increased their loans to Chile, concealing the extent of the economy's problems for a little longer. The trade deficit meanwhile continued to widen, and the scale of Chile's foreign indebtedness reached alarming proportions. By the end of 1981, repayments on it were taking a staggering 81 per cent of Chile's export earnings. The bulk of this money was owned by Chile's private sector, contracted in the heady days of government 'non-intervention' in bankers' affairs.

At the end of 1981, the Santiago chamber of commerce warned that bad loans, those unpaid 30 days after the fixed time of repayment, had reached dangerous levels. The process of automatic adjustment to the recession had led to high interest rates and an epidemic of major bankruptcies. There were clear signs that the inflow of foreign loans was drying up. Unemployment was soaring, close to 18 per cent if one added those on the minimum employment programme to official figures.

In November, four banks and finance companies went bankrupt. They were not key parts of Chile's business empires, but the link between their failure and the difficulties industrial and agricultural concerns were experiencing from the recession was clear. Nevertheless, the government arrested three financiers involved in the debacle and took the banks over, declaring at the same time its faith in the process of 'automatic adjustment'. Few now believed it.

Something had to give. In April 1982, the chief designer of the Chicago model and the driving force behind it, Sergio de Castro, was sacked as minister of finance by Pinochet. But Pinochet himself was so closely tied to the model that De Castro was replaced by one of his own disciples, Sergio de la Cuadro, who could only promise 'greater flexibility'. 'Greater flexibility' meant devaluation of the peso, which finally came in June, accompanied by the trimmings of a typical Chicago package: reductions in wages and an increase in privatization of the remaining state sector companies. Devaluation itself solved nothing, being too little and too late. Inflation soon wiped out any of the benefits which might have accrued to Chile's exporters through the devaluation, and with interest rates rising locally and internationally, the banks' bad debts problem increased.

Policies became increasingly panic-stricken. In August 1982, the government was forced to take over the private banks' bad debt portfolios. The Chicago Boys' contribution to Chile's economy could now be seen as one of privatized profits and socialized losses. The peso was allowed to float, and immediately depreciated 40 per cent against the dollar.

The economy was now handed over to another Chicago graduate, Rolf Lüders, called in from the BHC business empire to help the president because no other economic team in Chile would supply a reputable economist without demanding significant political changes in return. Lüders became minister of both finance and the economy. He faced a daunting panorama: rising inflation, the GNP expected to fall by 12 per cent, and unemployment close to 30 per cent if the figures for PEM were included. Meanwhile, Doonie Edwards personally took over the task of editing *El Mercurio*, bulwark of the Chicago model, allowing no one else to interpret his real business interests. It was the end of an era.

In the south of Chile, the stronghold of Chile's fascist movements for three generations, former Fatherland and Freedom activist Roberto Thieme was forming a movement in opposition to the government, the Popular Nationalist Movement. His efforts culminated in October 1982 with 'The Declaration of Temuco', an open attack on the government's economic policies which Thieme himself hoped would spark off a military coup. Thieme had evidently not taken into account 'Allende's Law', that military governments are much less easy to remove from power than they are to install (See Box Page 101). The declaration had little immediate political impact, but it did produce one of the period's most curious political watersheds — the explicit disassociation of a local fascist group from the doctrine of National Security. Thieme now blamed this doctrine for the failure of the armed forces to intervene.

At the beginning of 1983 farce took over, with the final collapse of the Chilean banking system. Pinochet had already denounced the activities of bankers in December 1982, when he loudly proclaimed: 'I should have deported 100, no 200, of these paper emperors . . .' In January 1983, the government took over direct management control of nine key banks and finance houses, including the *Banco de Chile* of BHC and the *Banco de Santiago* of Cruzat-Larrain. The intervention was made necessary, in Lüders' own words, because of 'the magnitude of the expected portfolio losses'. Foreign bankers were assured that the government's general bias towards the private sector would continue, and the banks would be turned over to private management once the emergency ended. A subsequent government investigation revealed that by the end of September 1982, the total debt of Vial's *Banco de Chile* stood at 30 million pesos, of which 20 million had gone into Vial's own companies. Many of these loans were to 'paper companies without genuine activities or real guarantees'. Chile, it turned out, had been a speculator's paradise.

Allende's Law

A month before the coup, Allende forced me to attend a private meeting with himself and General Prats, with whom he insisted he had the closest of relationships. He insisted; so after enormous problems and precautions — it was a very tense moment, we're talking about the end of July, beginning of August 1973, I had breakfast with him. It was a dramatic moment, more so than you can imagine.

We were talking about a kind of project he had, a pact which he hoped would bring peace to the country.

So I said to him: 'But Mr President, you have nothing to offer. It's a waste of time to make a pact with you. You're a living corpse, you're useless. No politician with a minimal degree of skill will make a pact with you, for the simplest of reasons; he doesn't need to.'

So he said to me: 'You're convinced that the military will throw me out.'

'Yes,' I said, 'You'll fall as a result of a military coup, now, in a period of days, weeks, that's the period.'

So he said to me: 'You think,' he said, 'that the military in Chile will organize a coup in order to save the large landowners or the investments of the rich?'

No,' I said, 'they won't do it for that; or at least they won't think that's why they're doing it. They'll do it for order, security, the values they believe in, for social peace, for the internal and external security of this country. Or at least, that's what they'll believe . . .'

Well,' he said, 'that means civil war.'

'No,' I said, 'You're very wrong there. There won't be any civil war, Mr President, you will fall without pain and without glory. There won't be anyone beside you when it happens, and you'll have to hunt hard to find one of those 43 per cent of the votes which you won in that last election. And everyone will be asking, ''Where's that 43 per cent who voted for you only two months ago?'' Because that's the nature of the Chilean people, that's their nature. The day you fall there won't be a single one beside you. No one, absolutely no one.'

So he came over to me, and he poured me a drink. And he said, 'I don't think so. But suppose you are right, let me tell you a couple of things. One, I, this thing here', and he touched himself, 'this is the flesh which statues are made of. I shall have statues carved to me and streets named after me. And not just in Santiago. You can have them here, so can Frei, but I shall have them in every capital of the world. There will be a street and a statue in Paris and one in Moscow and one in Peking and one in London, everywhere. And that will be my ultimate justification.'

'Let me tell you something else. You are looking for a military dictatorship. And from somewhere, not that I believe there's anything after death, but still, if there is, I shall look down on you all and find you all together, casting about for ways to get out of power the military man you replace me with. I shall see you all there, plotting and planning it, but with a great deal more difficulty than you are having now, how to get rid of the soldier you put in my place. *Because it won't cost you much to get him in. But by heaven, it will cost you something to get him out!'*

Seven years have passed since that meeting: and I think he may have been closer to the truth than I ever supposed.

Interview with Orlando Saenz, Chile, 1980.

Source: *Hoy* 24 March 1982

The Emergence of Mass Opposition

In early 1983, the copper workers took the enormously important step of calling all sectors of Chile's labour movement to form a new, united trade union confederation, without party loyalties, the National Workers Command *(Comando Nacional de Trabajadores)*. Gestures of unity promoted by one or other of the 'old hands' had always foundered in the past, shipwrecked on old political grievances or the pull of powerful international loyalties. But the 'old hands' were no longer running Chile's labour movement, and the new ones were facing an impatient rank and file.

A national strike fund was to be created. The new confederation would also seriously consider organizing solidarity strikes with workers in industry unable to preserve their jobs or their wage levels in the face of the existing economic model and the legal restrictions on bargaining. Workers in the factories around Santiago had been voicing a demand for such actions since 1981. The copper workers, in the most powerful economic position possible within an export economy, were prepared to consider giving them support.

In March 1983 too, a cross-section of Chile's old politicians published a 'Democratic Manifesto' which called for an end to the Pinochet dictatorship, the restoration of the electoral system and a constituent assembly, the return of the exiles and an end to human rights abuses. It was signed by individuals from the Christian Democrat Party, the Social Democrat Party (the old PIR — Radical

103

Left Party), the National Party and three factions of the Socialist Party; the MIR and the Communist Party were excluded.

In April, the copper workers' congress issued a call for an indefinite national strike, not over any specific economic grievance but because 'it is a question of a complete economic, social, cultural and political system which is surrounding and crushing us . . . The time has come to stand up and say, enough!'

The Pinochet government responded with arrests and threats of worse military repression, and the US ambassador used his considerable influence with the 'old hands' in the Group of Ten to have the general strike called off. Nevertheless, in its place the copper workers called a series of national days of protest to begin on 11 May and to be held on the same day of every month thereafter until the government fell.

On 11 May students took to the streets and barricades were erected in Santiago's shanty-towns. Housewives banged their empty pots in a deliberate evocation of the December 1971 demonstration and motorists (popular myth has it, even Javier Vial himself), sounded their horns in protest against the government. Two youths died, and hundreds were arrested in clashes with the police. The 'old hands' of Chile's trade union right began to recognize the force of an overwhelming historical reality, and the UDT, the Catholic FUT and white-collar CEPCH took steps towards joining the *Comando Nacional de Trabajadores*. The CNS had seen the emergence of a new reality much earlier, and suggested to its rank and file supporters that they join the *Comando* in March 1983.

The June protest, actually held on 14 June, was a repeat of the May one, but bigger and more openly political. General Leigh himself visited the headquarters of the *Comando Nacional de Trabajadores* to offer his support. Workers and students organized silent and carefully 'non-violent' sit-ins at their place of work. Many schools were half empty, public transport was almost at a stand still, and housewives from the shanty-towns to the upper class suburbs banged their saucepans. As in May there was the odd explosion, and buses were burnt, and as in the previous month the police attempted to control the shanty-towns with brute force, killing two more people and arresting more than a thousand.

Pinochet, who left Santiago to avoid hearing the new protests of the 'women of Chile', made a typically unyielding declaration. 'If the protest demonstrations continue, the government will harden its position, whatever that may cost.' On the night of 14 June the president of the copper workers, Rodolfo Seguel, was kidnapped and taken into custody. From prison he smuggled out a note calling on workers to overcome their fear, and saying that the dictatorship was vulnerable. The *Comando* rejected efforts by the CEPCH, the UDT and others to negotiate a deal with the government behind its back. Copper workers went on strike until he was released, although the government threatened mass dismissal. The dismissals were carried out, but subsequently revoked. Seguel was released.

In July, the protesters were even better organized. The *Comando* was now a focus for every shade of opposition to the government. In spite of a curfew and the first use of the army to quell demonstrations since the coup, people took to the streets *en masse*. Three died, all teenage girls. Many were wounded. In a desperate attempt to defuse the protests, Pinochet had ordered the arrest of Christian Democrat leaders, including the party's president, Gabriel Valdes. They were charged with publishing and distributing 700,000 handbills, but this charge was squashed by the court of appeal. It was one of the first acts of independence from government dictates shown by the Chilean judiciary in a decade. Pinochet was seen to be increasingly vulnerable. Foreign bankers began to feel the need to investigate the views of the opposition.

10 The Model in Retrospect

Dead End for Chicago

The story of the Pinochet decade is the story of an alliance between Pinochet, the respectable media, and the new *laissez-faire* economic technicians, the Nobel Prize winners of their generation. It is a very modern story, which perhaps makes it even uglier.

The Chicago Boys were hardly responsible for the mass violence which surrounded the coup, nor even perhaps for the coup itself. The takeover of power by the Chilean military in 1973 was masterminded by the United States and a few Chilean businessmen. The violence was a result largely of the military's own 'professional' training, mostly by the United States in the doctrine of National Security. But the Chicago Boys, and those who taught them, do have a large measure of responsibility for what has happened since.

'Shock', for instance, was their decision. With the active support of Milton Friedman and Arnold Harberger, who used their international influence to help the project along, the Chicago Boys took the opportunity of a temporary balance of payments crisis to introduce a social, cultural, political as well as economic revolution in Chile. Before the coup, Chile was clearly the kind of society they loathed. Its strong moral instincts, powerful syndicalist and corporate traditions, high-minded men insisting on some kind of national economic development and 57 varieties of democratic politician were the worst kind of vices to men like Hayek. He detected them also in Britain when he wrote his political manifesto, *1980s: Unemployment and the Unions*. 'Shock' was introduced in a deliberate attempt to replace a society based on those vices with another type of society altogether.

The Chicago model is based on one extraordinarily simple idea: the argument that economic liberty is more fundamental than political liberty. From this idea two disturbing conclusions are drawn. One conclusion is that national economies are dangerous, because they can in principle be controlled by the deliberate intervention of high-minded politicians. The other is that all political institutions should be structured in such a way as to leave no room for any human intervention in economic affairs which might disrupt the workings of the market. The first principle gives us the open economy, the second a series of restrictions on political freedom, ranging from constitutional prohibitions on union closed shops, to that whole spectrum of constitutional arrangements known as 'authoritarian democracy'.

The open economy meant, in Chile, the destruction of most of the country's local industries and a reversion to the typical profile of a 'banana economy' dependent on exports of primary products processed by cheap labour. The Chicago Boys were quite willing to pay that price, perhaps because like the oligarchy of old, they belonged to the social groups whose standard of living would rise if tariff barriers went down and the prices of manufactured goods slumped.

During the boom years, the model was financed by international bankers, through a flood of loans based on little more than political fellow-feeling, which floated an economy substantially more prosperous than the model should have allowed. Those years gave the Chicago Boys a chance to introduce Chile's poor to cheap transistor radios, and promised them a consumer revolution which would make all the sacrifices worthwhile. But what happens when the flow of loans is contracted, and the price of primary goods on world markets drops? The Chicago model assumes that adjustment will be automatic, meaning that Chile's workers and its poor would bear the brunt of the cost. The new *laissez-faire* is profoundly reactionary in its attempt to institutionalize the class privileges of the few by dismantling all those reforms which have given the majority some protection against the savagery of an open market. As the Catholic Church has consistently said since 1975, it is an unchristian philosophy which recognizes only demands based on income, and never needs, and which sees labour as a factor of production with a price to be determined entirely by the market, no different from machines.

The new *laissez-faire* involves more suffering for most people in a world which, the economic text-books tell us, has a surplus of labour. Therefore it involves major increases in state power in at least one area, the surveillance of dissent and repression. Democratic and popular advances through the state are something the model has ruled

107

out, by definition. But such advances have been made in the past. Therefore the state has to intervene in the minds of its citizens to prohibit them from considering further advances in this direction as a real political possibility. The Constitution of Liberty is quite clear in its prescriptions. 'Totalitarian' ideas have to be banned from the framework of 'democracy'. People who mention them in public are to be disenfranchised, and if they take any further steps to put them into effect, they will ultimately fall into the hands of the secret police. A more totalitarian recipe, in practice, would have been difficult to invent.

It was in the interests of precisely this kind of system that the Chicago Boys consistently supported the forces which were thrusting Chile towards a total centralization of power in the hands of one man, Pinochet. That was not the only model available in South America for armed forces exercising power. In comparative terms, it is even rather unusual, for elsewhere national security regimes have seen some kind of collegiate military control over the state, with presidents rotating periodically and the armed forces, if no one else, having the right to an open political debate. But absolutism was the system which best served Chicago interests. Elsewhere in Latin America, the experiments have been much less extreme.

In retrospect, the story of Chile since 1973 is a story of the defeat of this model at the hands of the popular organizations which it mobilized so effectively to bring it to power. Its heroes are the unions and the *gremios*, textile workers, dockers, copper miners, taxi-drivers, shopkeepers, truckers and doctors. They are not saints, and collectively they bear a considerable responsibility for the failure of Chile to agree on a developmental path which would have met the needs of the majority of its population, from 1964 to 1973. Hayek is right in some instances to regard them as privileged groups. And it is true that in a society of massive unemployment, these are all groups which have only two options open to them if they want to preserve their traditional living standards; to raise a barrier of privilege between themselves and the unemployed, or on the other hand, to work for a society in which the worst social conditions are tackled through an active, political choice to mitigate the effects of the market. In practice they do both. The Chicago model tried to prevent them from doing either, and it failed.

Democracy and its Limits

The principle of limited democracy is essentially that the great mass of citizens shall accept that they have no right to act as political agents, and leave that area to a very privileged few. It is not an order which defends the underprivileged. It was an order which ensured the Chicago Boys their basic salary of 80,000 pesos plus interest from shares, while proposing that dockers should have theirs cut from 20,000 to 3,000 and student doctors should work in private clinics for free, because the market had indicated an excess supply. It is an order which attempts, at all costs, to prohibit any notion that economics should be re-ordered in the interests of social justice.

As such, the Chicago model was never a very probable future for Chile, where first the Marxists and then the Catholic Church, in the best traditions of free competition, have been busily engaged in stitching together an enormously dense patchwork of popular organizations for four generations. Chile has always been a highly politicized society, a place where the local fire station is run by the Radicals, Socialists and Christian Democrats run the local Mother's Union and elections for shop steward at a factory of 200 workers offer a choice between candidates from the Communists, the Socialists, the Christian Democrats and the Christian Left. It is a society which values political choice, political freedom and the idea of a social conscience very highly.

Had it not been for the enormous violence of the coup itself, which wiped out many of the individuals involved in this extraordinary deep and fertile rank and file network there would never have been any question of Chile applying a Hayekian model. As it was, Pinochet drew the inevitable conclusion in 1980, when he took on board the Chicago Boys 'modernization' policy and followed it with a political constitution which enshrined his own arbitrary powers and the reign of terror. Only increased repression could make this system work.

Since then, the experience of Chile has proved that a sufficiently well-rooted democracy, one with a network of local political representatives covering every office, every church, every street corner, every newspaper kiosk and every mine and factory, can take on a totalitarian system and make it back down. In this, the message of Chile is not very different from that of Poland. People want to determine their own futures, not have them determined by an elite which considers that its ideology or its status as a science gives it the right to total power. And if they are strong enough, and determined enough, over a long enough period of time, then ultimately they will win.

Appendix: Human Rights and the Pinochet Decade

Jon Barnes, of the Chile Committee for Human Rights

It is difficult to ascertain the exact number of people who lost their lives following the 1973 coup. Reliable estimates put the figure as high as 30,000. An unofficial report of the US State Department indicated 10,800 people had been killed by December 1973. In the first month after the coup people were summarily executed following court martials convened on the spot by the local military commanders. Cooperation or mere association with the Allende government warranted the charge of high treason. Legal protection was non-existent and the ministers of the Supreme Court declared that they had no jurisdiction over the military tribunals as long as the state of siege lasted. It is estimated that over 150,000 people were arrested after the coup and over 20,000 were held as political prisoners in military premises, on naval ships, in prisons or in special detention centres such as the national football stadium in Santiago. Concentration camps were set up throughout the country. Many prisoners were interrogated, executed, beaten or tortured to·death. Bodies of prisoners were found in the River Mapocho. Methods of torture included burning with cigarettes or acid, the application of electricity to sensitive parts of the body, beatings with rifle butts, rape, and being forced to eat excrement.

In the first few weeks after the coup repression was widespread, arbitrary and indiscriminate. After a period, however, repression became more coordinated and centralized. Perhaps the best expression of this development was the creation in June 1974 of a secret police force, the Directorate of National Intelligence (DINA). A subordinate body of the military junta, the DINA was to last until August 1977 and was directly responsible for the purging of all the political opponents of the military regime.

Between 1973 and 1977 the DINA was responsible for the 'disappearance' of over 2,000 Chileans. They were kidnapped from their homes, in the street, or at their place of work, and taken to secret detention centres for interrogation under torture. Most were never heard of again. In over 650 cases of missing persons, there is strong circumstantial evidence and witnesses to corroborate their arrest and detention in the centres belonging to the DINA. The courts have been unable, or unwilling, to investigate the activities of the security forces and only four of the 5,000 *habeas corpus* petitions presented on behalf of the missing prisoners have been accepted. In a few cases bodies have been found and the courts have been able to positively identify them as previously 'disappeared' people as well as to establish the names of members of the security forces responsible for their death. Nevertheless, the judges have declared themselves incompetent to intervene and when the matter has been passed on to the military courts they have inevitably absolved those responsible for these crimes. They invoke the 1978 amnesty which granted an official pardon for atrocities committed by the security forces after the coup as well as affecting political prisoners of the regime. Throughout this period thousands of people were forced to leave the country while hundreds upon hundreds lost their jobs for political reasons.

The systematic violation of human rights by the Pinochet regime was strongly condemned by the international community. Chile's human rights record was investigated by the Organization of American States' Inter-American Commission on Human Rights and in 1975, following several condemnatory resolutions of the UN General Assembly, the United Nations Commission on Human Rights set up an Ad Hoc Working Group to examine the regime's record. Chile also became the object of fierce criticism from other countries. In Britain, the Labour government of the time broke off diplomatic relations and imposed an arms embargo on the junta after the torture of the British doctor, Sheila Cassidy. In the United States, despite the support for the Pinochet regime from the Nixon and Ford administrations, several liberal congressmen successfully increased controls on the flow of arms to Chile. In 1976, the Kennedy Amendment banned all military aid to Chile. For its part, the Carter administration pressured the Pinochet regime, calling for the extradition of DINA agents implicated in the murder of Orlando Letelier in 1976.

International pressure did have some important effects. For example, the practice of long term mass 'disappearances' had virtually stopped by 1977. However, by then so many opposition leaders were dead, imprisoned, or in exile, and the civilian population terrorized, that this kind of repression was no longer required to maintain order. Serious human rights violations continued in the form of selective repression. A few cosmetic changes were made for international consumption. The number of political prisoners was reduced by sending them into exile, the DINA was dissolved and replaced by a more 'technical' secret police force, the CNI, and the state of siege was replaced by a state of emergency.

The institutionalization of repression

In September 1980, a plebiscite was held on the new constitution. Despite numerous irregularities (documented by the International Commission of Jurists and others) Pinochet managed to win over 60 per cent of the vote and in March 1981 the transition period of the new constitution came into effect.

The transition period established a new dual state of emergency which conferred on General Pinochet wide-ranging and exceptional powers, similar to those which had existed under the state of siege. Article 24 of the new constitution for example allows people to be held *incomunicado* for up to 20 days without charge. It is during this period of short term 'disappearance', often in the secret detention centres of the CNI, that torture occurs. Article 24 also gave Pinochet the right to expel people from the country, deny them entry, or to banish people to inhospitable parts of the country (internal exile) for up to three months. All these measures can be carried out by administrative decree, that is without the right to appeal to a court of law.

As well as infringing individual human rights the new constitution institutionalizes previous decree laws which violate basic civil and political rights. Article 10, for example legalizes the 'political recess' by declaring party political activity illegal.

The institutionalization of repression through the new constitution took place in a particular context: the project of Pinochet and his allies to restructure the Chilean economy and to redefine the Chilean state. Just as there is a single, basic authoritarian and coercive political ideology behind the new constitution, the particular economic model launched by the military regime is also enshrined in law as the only model admissible. Thus while several clauses in the constitution legalize the violation of individual, civil and political rights, many parts of the text, which refer to the establishment of the new economic order, are at odds with international statutes governing social and economic rights. Rather than guarantee the 'right to work' as in the previous 1925 constitution, the new constitution refers to the 'freedom to work'. It embodies in law the idea that the availability of work should be regulated by market forces and that the state no longer has responsibility for ensuring work for everyone. The right to social services had previously been formally recognized in Chile. In the new constitution, the state merely declares that it will supervise those bodies, public or private, which are responsible for the provision of social services. Since 1975, the state in Chile has in fact increasingly withdrawn from these particular areas. The implications of these shifts can be seen in labour rights, housing, social security and health and education.

Labour rights

Following years of repression and a direct ban on the right to strike, the Labour Plan was announced in 1979. Although the new labour laws verbally recognized trade union rights such as the right to strike or the right of unions to elect their own officials, these rights are tightly restricted by regulations which are at variance with international labour statutes (e.g. those of the International Labour Organization). Indeed, the right to strike and collective bargaining are limited to factory level. Thus only the trade union of the factory concerned and not a federation or confederation representing an industry as a whole can negotiate with an employer. 'Solidarity strikes' are therefore ruled out. Strikes can only be called in support of wage or other economic demands and can only last for 59 days, after which the management has the right to replace all the striking workforce. Even during the permitted strike period, the management may hire replacement labour. Whereas during strikes employers pay no tax or wages, the workforce must continue to pay tax. Under new provisions since 1981, the Labour Plan gives the employer the right to sack ten per cent of his workforce monthly. It is therefore not uncommon for workers to be sacked and then rehired at lower rates of pay. The abolition of industrial tribunals in 1981 has meant that workers are virtually left unprotected by law. The legislation is aimed at excluding workers from the discussion of wider issues affecting their interests, such as national economic policy. The labour laws aim to fragment the labour force and eliminate its right to express any political view.

The right to shelter

Monetarist economics have had a series effect on the right of the people to adequate shelter. The shortage of housing in Chile has always been a problem, yet governments before 1973 attempted to deal with it through initiatives such as the creation of the national housing service which took on a major role within the construction industry. Since then, however, despite the fact that the government itself has admitted that over 800,000 people are homeless or inadequately housed, the military regime has turned over responsibility for the provision of housing to market forces and abolished the government housing service. As the housing minister stated in 1980: '. . . The government has no obligation to give housing . . .' Consequently, the demand for housing has been determined by one's ability (or inability) to pay. When no demand came, the regime decided in 1978 to inject some dynamism into the market by setting up a loan scheme for families wishing to buy property. With 30 per cent unemployment in 1983 and with a quarter of the national workforce employed on the government's PEM earning US$35 a month (in a country where the cost of living is only slightly less than in Britain), few of those in desperate need of housing can afford to pay the monthly loans. It is only those with relatively high wage levels who can participate in the government's subsidy programme. In spite of the urgent need for housing, the boom in the construction industry between 1978 and 1980 was primarily directed towards the building of luxury apartments and extravagant commercial centres, the latter to sell all kinds of luxury goods imported from abroad as a result of the lowering of tariff barriers. The construction boom has however been short-lived; in 1983, 60 per cent of building workers were unemployed.

The right to social security and health

Similar developments have taken place in the areas of social security and health. The dismantling of the Chilean social security system in 1980 ended one of the most comprehensive systems in Latin America which had benefited some 68 per cent of the population, providing health care, pensions and unemployment benefit. The new private scheme managed by the pension fund administration companies favours those with higher wages who can afford the payments and ends the principle of 'social solidarity' on which the old system had been based. Indeed, many of the low paid or the unemployed cannot afford cover under the new scheme because they are unable to pay the rates demanded. Moreover, following the gradual dismantling of the Chilean national health service (established in 1952), the pension fund companies also handle payments to the new private health care institutes. Two kinds of medical service have been established in Chile, a technical and high cost private care system based on private health insurance, and orientated to those who can pay, and a run-down and under-financed national health service for the poor and destitute who can afford nothing else. Since 1975 the national health service has had its budget cut, and in 1979 the service was decentralized and divided into 27 regional health authorities which were given responsibility for providing the most basic health care at the local level.

Health and social security, rather than being automatic social rights related to need, are now part of the profit-making strategies of those large Chilean firms which control the pension fund administration companies. According to figures for 1981, 61 per cent of clients belonged to pension funds administered by the two largest economic groups in Chile which, at the time, owned nearly 50 per cent of private capital assets in the country. This implies that health and social security provision has become dependent on the financial success of these companies.

The right to education

The policy of regional reorganization has been crucial to the aims and objectives of the economic and political 'modernizations' carried out by the regime from 1979 onwards. In line with the regime's free market economic policy, the decentralization of education is intended to make local authorities responsible for the organization, administration and eventually the financing of education in their areas. Rather than organizing the whole system, the ministry of education's role is now limited to the licensing of private education and the carrying out of school inspections. Any belief that the decentralization of education would entail the relaxation of political control by the regime was mistaken. It is now the local mayors, the *alcaldes* (who are appointed by General Pinochet and responsible to the provincial military commander) who have absolute authority over the administration of education in their area. The transfer of responsibility for the provision of education to the *alcaldes* has had several consequences. Inevitably, rich areas find it easy to provide their own education on a local level whether it be private or public, while poorer areas have had serious difficulties. Moreover, the unavoidable problems of managing such a system on a local level have meant that the *alcalde* has preferred to pass on responsibility to third parties, and this has encouraged the privatization of education.

Although the state still assumes responsibility for some primary education, all other education has to be paid for. Breaking the concept of 'equality of opportunity' and 'equality of access' which had prevailed in Chile until 1973, the regime now sees progress to secondary or higher education as the 'exception' rather than the rule. Indeed, one part of the Decree Law 4002 which established the modernization in education states: 'It is most important that the teacher is absolutely convinced that people deserve and are happy in what they are and not in what they do or possess. Only then is it possible to give orientation to many of the children in our schools and not to raise false hopes. Insist from primary school level that only the most outstanding will go to university . . .' Decree Law 4002 also establishes a course called 'Education in Freedom'. This states that: 'A child often has to live in a situation which he has not chosen and he must try to freely accept it. For example, physical handicap, illness, family tragedy and problems of fortune. Teaching should help the child to accept this situation as this is an important factor in the balanced development of a child.' As well as teaching children their social position in the new economic order, the compulsory basic primary education provided by the state orientates them as to what their political views should be. 'Particular emphasis will be given in history to the formation of the Chilean nationality and its people; national unity, great military, economic, cultural, and civil events of our country and people, with emphasis placed on individual values, especially of those who have sacrificed their lives and interests in the service of the fatherland.'

An examination of the recent aspects of the military regime's education policy is particularly fruitful since it provides a microcosmic image of the kind of economic, political and social order which the regime has attempted to forge and demonstrates quite clearly how the economic model, political control, and the violation of human rights all intertwine.

The present human rights situation

'It is a question of a complete economic social and political system which is crushing us and which goes against our nature as Chileans and workers, which has tried to trap us ever more deeply with the weapons of fear and repression. If we do not fight for changes we would be betraying our democratic union principles. The time has come to stand up and say: enough . . .'

Declaration of the Chilean Copper Workers Confederation April 1983.

Since 1981 the catastrophic economic collapse in Chile has created the most serious political crisis for the Pinochet regime, and this has effected not just the human rights situation but also the way the human rights problem is now seen by Chileans.

The deepening of the economic crisis has seen a corresponding deterioration in the human rights situation in Chile. In 1982, the UN General Assembly condemned the systematic violation of human rights in Chile for the ninth year in succession. That year there was a sharp increase in the number of arbitrary arrests, the reported cases of torture and extrajudicial killings. The figures for arrests of political dissidents in 1982 were double those for 1981, and the figures for 1983 will more than double those for 1982. Several mass protest demonstrations have taken place against the military government in 1983, and during the national protests of May and June 1983 called by the copper workers and other trade unions, thousands of arrests were made all over the country. The response of the regime to these challenges has been one of mass repression, in scenes which are reminiscent of the early years after the military coup in 1973. In a reprisal operation for the first national protest of 11 May, the secret police, military police and the military arrested 1,400 people in a mass raid on several shanty-towns in Santiago and held them on a football pitch, now converted into an improvised concentration camp. One person was tortured in public with an electric prod.

Nevertheless, the Pinochet regime is now rapidly losing the political initiative, and long term political gains from such repression are far lower than they were in the past. Sectors which had given the regime unconditional support in the past are now criticizing some aspects of its arbitrary rule, particularly as they have come to experience it themselves. In December 1982 for example, the president of the wheat producers association, Carlos Podlech, was expelled from the country with two other trade union leaders from the CNS. The expulsion of Podlech had a considerable impact on conservative sectors in Chile. For the first time they began to discuss issues such as the unjust nature of measures under article 24 of the constitution which had permitted the expulsion of someone from their own social class by administrative decree. Indeed, in 1982 the question of the estimated one million Chilean exiles abroad became a national issue.

As the Pinochet decade draws to a close, the issue of human rights is once again on the agenda. The systematic violation of human rights underpinned the 'success' of the Chicago model. Now, as the model collapses, the government is having once again to resort to violence and repression to sustain its arbitrary rule. But this time Pinochet faces a broad opposition movement that is making respect for human rights one of their central demands.

Bibliography

Chile Committee for Human Rights, *Pinochet's Chile, An Eyewitness Report,* 1981.

Andre Gunder Frank, *Economic Genocide in Chile: Monetarist Theory versus Humanity (Two Open Letters to Arnold Harberger and Milton Friedman),* Spokesman Books, 1976.

Colin Henfrey and Bernard Sorj, *Chilean Voices,* Harvester Press, 1977.

Ian Roxborough, Phil O'Brien and Jackie Roddick, *Chile: The State and Revolution,* Macmillan, 1977.

Stefan de Vylder, *Chile 1970-73: The Political Economy of the Rise and Fall of the Unidad Popular,* Cambridge University Press, 1977.

World University Service, *Education and Repression,* Chile, 1982.

Ann J. Zammit (ed), *The Chilean Road to Socialism,* Sussex University, 1973.

THE CHILE COMMITTEE FOR HUMAN RIGHTS

The Chile Committee for Human Rights (CCHR) was set up in January 1974 following the military coup of 1973. It campaigns for the full restoration of human rights, individual rights, civil and political rights, and social and economic rights in Chile. Over the past decade, CCHR has taken up issues such as torture, arbitrary killings and arrest, the plight of the 'disappeared', and the situation of political prisoners. CCHR has also campaigned on the drastic social consequences of the regime's policies which have violated rights to education, to health, to work and to trade union and political organization. CCHR presses the British government to demonstrate its concern over the human rights situation in Chile and informs the British public of the current situation on the basis of frequent fact-finding missions to the country.

CCHR materials include

- A bi-monthly newsletter, (£5 for individuals, £7 overseas, £8 organizations)
- *'Pinochet's Chile: an Eyewitness Report'* (£1.50 incl. p&p).
- An Education Pack *'Human Rights in the Southern Cone'* (£2.50 incl. p&p).
- Two tape-slide shows for hire (£5 per week)
  'The Military's New Chile'
  'Fight for Survival of the Mapuche Indians'

For further information please contact:
CCHR, 266 Pentonville Road, London N1.
Tel: 01-837 7561